WHAT THE BEST COLLEGE TEACHERS DO

WHAT THE
BEST COLLEGE
TEACHERS
DO

Ken Bain

HARVARD UNIVERSITY PRESS

Cambridge, Massachusetts

London, England

Library of Congress Cataloging-in-Publication Data
Bain, Ken.
What the best college teachers do / Ken Bain.
   p. cm.
Includes bibliographical references and index.
ISBN 0-674-01325-5 (alk. paper)
1. College teaching—United States. 2. Effective teaching—United States.
I. Title.
LB2331.B34 2004
378.1'2—dc22   2003062869

To the memory of my parents, my first teachers

CONTENTS

WHAT THE BEST COLLEGE TEACHERS DO

INTRODUCTION:
DEFINING THE BEST

When Ralph Lynn graduated from college in 1932, decked out in a variety of academic honors, he began doing other people's laundry to survive the depression. Ten years later, he acquired a correspondence-course teaching certificate and taught high school history classes for six months before entering the army in late 1942. He spent most of World War II in London looking at other people's dirty laundry—censoring soldiers' letters to keep them from revealing too much about troop movements to the folks back home—and reading history. When he came home in 1945, he asked his alma mater, Baylor University, to let him teach. Later, he went north to the University of Wisconsin to acquire a Ph.D. in European history. In 1953 he returned to Texas, where he taught for the next twenty-one years.

When Lynn retired in 1974, more than one hundred of his former students who now held academic posts paid him tribute. One of them, Robert Fulghum, who later wrote a much celebrated book claiming that he learned everything he needed to know about life in kindergarten, confessed that Ralph Lynn was the "best teacher in the world." Another student, Ann Richards, who became the governor of Texas in 1991, wrote that Lynn's classes "offered us a window to the world, and for a young girl from Waco, his classes were great adventures." They were, she explained some years after leaving the governor's mansion, like "magical tours into the great minds and movements of history." Hal Wingo, who took classes from Lynn long before he became the editor of *People* magazine, concluded that Lynn offered the best argument he knew for human cloning. "Nothing would give me more hope for the future," the editor explained, "than to think that Ralph Lynn, in all his wisdom and wit, will be around educating new generations from here to eternity."[1]

What did Lynn do to have such a sustained and substantial influence on the intellectual and moral development of his students? What do any of the best college and university teachers do to help and encourage students to achieve remarkable learning results? What does Jeanette Norden, a professor of cell biology who teaches the brain to medical students at Vanderbilt University, do that enables her students to learn so deeply? How does Ann Woodworth, a professor of theater at Northwestern University, lift her acting students to heights of thespian brilliance? Given that human cloning is not an option, is it possible to do some intellectual cloning, to capture the thinking of people like Don Saari from the University of California at Irvine, whose calculus students have sometimes claimed 90 percent of the A's on departmental examinations? Can we capture the magic of Paul Travis and Suhail Hanna, who taught history and literature in a small freshwater college in Oklahoma in the 1970s and later at other institutions from Pennsylvania to Kansas, inspiring their students to new intellectual levels?

What makes some teachers successful with students of diverse backgrounds? Consider the case of Paul Baker, a teacher who spent nearly fifty years empowering his students to find their own creativity. In the 1940s Baker developed for an undergraduate theater program a course he called "Integration of Abilities," a mind-charging exploration of the creative process that attracted as many future engineers, scientists, and historians as it did actors and other artists. By the late 1950s, he used the course to build the graduate program in theater at the Dallas Theater Center and later at Trinity University, revolutionizing theater productions around the world. By the 1970s he was employing the integrations method as head of the new performing arts magnet high school in Dallas, changing the lives of many students whom others had dismissed as failures. In the early 1990s, now retired on a small ranch in East Texas, he took the same approach in creating a program for the local elementary school that pushed standardized test scores in that rural community to historic highs. How did he do it?

For more than fifteen years I have raised such questions in looking at the practices and thinking of the best teachers, those people who have remarkable success in helping their students achieve exceptional learning results. Much of the inspiration for the inquiry came from the extraordinarily successful teachers I have encountered in my own life. It has occurred to me that teaching is one of those human endeavors that seldom benefits from its past. Great teachers emerge, they touch the lives of their students, and perhaps only through some of those students do they have any influence on the broad art of teaching. For the most part, their insights die with them, and subsequent generations must discover anew the wisdom that drove their practices. At best, some small fragment of their talent endures, broken pieces on which later generations perch without realizing the full measure of the ancient wealth beneath them.

A decade ago, I confronted the tragedy of losing some of that wealth in the death of a talented teacher whom I never formally met. When I was a graduate student at the University of Texas in the early 1970s, I heard about a young professor, fresh from his own studies at the University of Chicago, who had students sitting in the aisles for the chance to take his class. Nearly every day, I saw a small army of people follow Tom Philpott from class to the departmental lounge, where they continued the conversations his teaching had started. In the late 1980s my son and daughter-in-law took Philpott's class in U.S. urban history, and I watched as it provoked new questions and perspectives. I listened with renewed interest to their stories of students—even many who were not registered for the class—who crowded into the legendary teacher's classroom for a charge to their intellectual batteries. I wanted to interview Philpott about his teaching and possibly videotape some classes, but that chance never came. A short while later he took his own life. His colleagues eulogized him, his students remembered his classes, and perhaps a few of them who became teachers carried some pieces of his talent into their own careers. But for the most part his library of teaching talents and practices burned to the ground when he died. His scholarship on the development of neighborhoods in Chicago remains, but he never captured his own scholarship of teaching, and no one else did it for him.

In this book I have tried to capture the collective scholarship of some of the best teachers in the United States, to record not just what they do but also how they think, and most of all, to begin to conceptualize their practices. The study initially included only a handful of teachers at two universities, but eventually it encompassed professors at two dozen institutions—from open admissions colleges to highly selective research universities. Some taught primarily students with the best academic credentials; others worked with students who had substandard school records. Altogether, my colleagues and I looked at the thinking and practices of between sixty and seventy teachers. We studied nearly three dozen of them extensively, the others, less exhaustively. A few of the latter subjects were speakers in one of the annual series I organized at Vanderbilt and Northwestern that featured professors from other institutions who had achieved impressive teaching results. The subjects came from both medical school faculties and undergraduate departments in a variety of disciplines, including the natural and social sciences, the humanities, and the performing arts. A few came from graduate programs in management, and two came from law schools. We wanted to know what outstanding professors do and think that might explain their accomplishments. Most important, we wanted to know if the lessons they taught us could inform other people's teaching. I have directed this book to people who teach, but its conclusions should also be of interest to students and their parents.

DEFINING EXCELLENCE

To begin this study we had to define what we meant by outstanding teachers. That turned out to be a fairly simple matter. All the professors we chose to put under our pedagogical microscope had achieved remarkable success in helping their students learn in ways that made a sustained, substantial, and positive influence on how those students think, act, and feel. The actual classroom performance of the teachers did not matter to us; so long as the teachers did not do their students (or anyone else) any harm in the process, we cared little about how they achieved their results. Dazzling lecture styles, lively classroom discussions, problem-based exercises, and popular field research or projects might or might not contribute to the *telos* of good teaching. Their presence or absence, however, never dictated which people we investigated. We chose teachers because they produced important educational results.

What counted as evidence that a professor profoundly helped and encouraged students to learn deeply and remarkably? That question proved to be more complex. No one type of evidence would do in every case. We simply looked for proof of an educator's excellence, and if we found it, we used that person in the study. In some cases the evidence came in clearly labeled packages; in others, we had to collect it from unmarked jars and piece it together like anthropologists in search of a lost civilization. The types of evidence available depended on both the individual and the discipline.

Jeanette Norden from Vanderbilt University's Medical School and Ann Woodworth from the Theatre Department at Northwestern illustrate two different patterns of evidence. Norden's medical students face a standardized test of their learning in the form of the National Board of Medical Examiners and the United States

Medical Licensing Examination. Their group performance on sections of the exam that cover Norden's field provides a strong indication of her students' learning. So does the students' testimony about how well her class prepared them for the rotation in neurology, the National Boards, and careers in medicine. So do the examinations she uses in her classes, carefully and rigorously constructed instruments that take students through specific cases that require extensive knowledge, advanced understanding, and sophisticated clinical reasoning skills. And so do her colleagues' statements about how well her students are prepared for subsequent work. Norden has won every award for teaching granted by the medical school and selected by the students—some of the awards more times than the university will now allow. When Vanderbilt's chancellor established endowed chairs of teaching excellence in 1993, Norden was the first recipient of that honor. In late 2000, the American Association of Medical Colleges presented her with its Robert Glaser award for teaching excellence.

Ann Woodworth also came with a plethora of teaching awards—including appointment to an endowed chair of teaching excellence at Northwestern. But those recognitions, while important and substantial, gave us no direct evidence about student learning. Woodworth's field certainly emphasizes student performance, but it has no standardized measure of dramatic accomplishments. What convinced us that her teaching was worthy of careful study? First, we had a large body of testimony from her students, not just that she was entertaining or witty, but that she helped them achieve substantial results. We were impressed with the consistency of the testimony, with the kinds of praise the students offered ("you'll learn more from her class than from any other at this school"; "this class changed my life"), and with the perfect marks they gave her in response to questions about stimulating intellectual interest and helping students learn. Second, we had considerable evidence about what Woodworth taught, information we gathered from her students, from her account of her courses, and from a term-long observation of one of her classes. Finally, we saw the performances of her students, both in final productions and in classroom work, in which her assistance often transformed a stale rendition into something magical.

Glowing reviews from students and colleagues alone were insufficient, however. We wanted indications from a variety of sources that a particular teacher was worthy of study. Although we did not insist that every instructor present exactly the same kinds of support, we did have two acid tests that all instructors had to meet before we included them in our final results.

First, we insisted on evidence that most of their students were highly satisfied with the teaching and inspired by it to continue to learn. This was no mere popularity contest; we were not interested in people because they were well liked by their students. Rather, we wanted indications from the students that the teacher had "reached them" intellectually and educationally, and had left them wanting more. We rejected the standards of a former dean who used to say, "I don't care if the students liked the class or not as long as they learned the material," which meant "I just want to see how they performed on the final." We too were concerned with how students performed on the final, but we had to weigh the growing body of evidence that students can "perform" on many types of examinations without changing their understanding or the way they subsequently think, act, or feel.[2] We were equally concerned with how they performed after the final. We were convinced that if students emerged from the class hating the experience, they were less likely to continue learning, or even to retain what they had supposedly gained from the class. A teacher might scare students into memorizing material for short-term recall by threatening punishment or imposing excessively burdensome workloads, but those tactics might also leave students traumatized by the experience and disliking the subject matter. Any teacher who causes students to hate the subject has certainly violated our principle of "do no harm."

We recognize that some professors might be enormously successful in helping a few students learn but far less so with most of them. Colleagues have told us about former professors who stimulated their intellectual development but left most students flat. These people obviously valued those mentors and sometimes even modeled their own careers after them, taking pride in what they saw as the elite cadre of their satisfied students, and perhaps even believing that alienation of the masses set them on a higher plane. Such professors may have great value for the academy, but they did not make our cut. We sought people who can make a silk purse out of what others might regard as a sow's ears, who constantly help their students do far better than anyone else expects.

Our second acid test concerned what students learned. This is tricky because it involved judgments about a variety of disciplines. We sought evidence that colleagues in the field or in closely related fields would regard the learning objectives as worthy and substantial. Yet we remained open to the possibility that some remarkable teachers developed highly valuable learning objectives that ignored the boundaries of the discipline and even, on occasion, offended many disciplinary purists—the medical school professor, for example, who integrated issues of personal and emotional development into a basic science class, helping to redefine the study of medicine. Indeed, most of the highly successful teachers in the study broke traditional definitions of courses, convincing us that success in helping students learn even some core material benefits from the teacher's willingness to recognize that human learning is a complex process. Thus we had to apply a sweeping sense of educational worth that stemmed not from any one discipline but rather from a broad educational tradition that values the liberal arts (including the natural sciences), critical thinking, problem solving, creativity, curiosity, concern with ethical issues, and both a breadth and depth of specific knowledge and of the various methodologies and standards of evidence used to create that knowledge.

In short, we included in our study only those teachers who showed strong evidence of helping and encouraging their students to learn in ways that would usually win praise and respect from both disciplinary colleagues and the broader academic community. But we also tried to include some educators who were operating on the fringes of current norms, defining learning wealth in important new ways. We also studied a few people who were highly successful with some classes and less so with others. For example, some teachers achieved wonderful results with large or small classes, advanced or beginning courses, but not with both. Such cases allowed us to make some comparisons between what worked and what did not.

We wanted to study teachers who had a sustained influence on their students, but the evidence for that proved difficult to obtain, especially in the early phases of our research. We talked with some students years after they had taken a particular professor and heard their testimonies about the way the class touched their minds and influenced their lives. We did not, however, systematically follow students; nor did we rely on those interviews alone to decide that someone deserved attention. Instead, we looked for something that would tell us more immediately that the impact was lasting. The concept of deep learners, first developed by Swedish theorists in the 1970s, helped us spot indications of sustained influence.[3]

We assumed that deep learning was likely to last, and so we listened closely for evidence of it in the language students used to describe their experiences. Did they speak about "learning the material" or about developing an understanding, making something their own, "getting into it," and "making sense of it all?" We were drawn to classes in which students talked not about how much they had to remember but about how much they came to understand

(and as a result remembered). Some students talked about courses that "transformed their lives," "changed everything," and even "messed with their heads." We looked for signs that students developed multiple perspectives and the ability to think about their own thinking; that they tried to understand ideas for themselves; that they attempted to reason with the concepts and information they encountered, to use the material widely, and to relate it to previous experience and learning. Did they think about assumptions, evidence, and conclusions?

Consider, for example, two sets of comments. One came from students who told us that the class "required a lot of work," that the professor motivated them to "get it done," and was thorough and fair, "covering," as one student put it, "all the stuff that would be on the exam" and "never surprising us with problems we hadn't seen." The students dwelled on being successful "in the course" and offered high praise because the instructor helped them achieve that goal. While these comments were all quite favorable, they did not necessarily point to deep learning. In contrast, the second set of students talked about how they could "put a lot of things together now" or "get inside" their own heads. They stressed that they wanted to learn more, sometimes spoke about changing majors to study under a particular professor, and seemed in awe of and fascinated with how much they didn't know. "I thought it was all cut and dried before I took this course," one student explained. "It's pretty exciting stuff." They talked about issues that the course had raised, how they learned to think differently, how the course had changed their lives, and what they planned to do with what they had learned. They easily discussed arguments they had encountered, questioned assumptions, and distinguished between evidence and conclusions. Students mentioned books they had subsequently read because the course raised their interest, projects they had undertaken, or changes in plans. In commenting about a math class one student explained, "He didn't just show us how to solve the problem but helped us think about it so we could do it on our own. I can think through problems better now." In reference to a history class, that reflection became, "I don't just memorize stuff in here. I have to think about arguments and evidence." The second set of comments suggested sustained influences while the first didn't tell us enough.

As our inquiry developed, it generated enormous interest from colleagues, who often suggested that we consider particular people. All potential subjects entered the study on probation while we examined their learning objectives and pressed them for evidence about success in fostering meaningful results. Sometimes we quietly dropped people from consideration, not because we came to believe that they were ineffective teachers, but because we just did not have enough data to know, one way or the other. My objective in this book is not to notify these colleagues who were not included in the study but to learn as much as possible from the most successful teachers. Consequently, though I mention the names of many people we analyzed, I do not provide a complete list.

CONDUCTING THE STUDY

Once we had identified our subjects, we studied them. Some we observed in the classroom, laboratory, or studio; others, we videotaped. For still others, we did both. We had long conversations with many of the teachers and their students; looked at course materials, including syllabi, examinations, assignment sheets, and even some lecture notes; considered examples of students' work; conducted what we called "small group analyses," in which we interviewed entire classes in small groups; asked some people to analyze and describe their own teaching practices and philosophies in more formal reflections; and in a few cases actually sat in on an entire course. The methods of collection and analysis varied, but they all came from approaches common in history, literary analysis, investigative journalism, and anthropology. The talks we heard, the interviews we conducted, the class materials and other writings we read, and the notes we took while observing a class formed the texts that we subsequently scrutinized (see the appendix for details on the study).

STUDENT RATINGS

Before turning to a summary of the major findings of our study, we should consider one more methodological issue: What role can student ratings play in helping identify outstanding teaching? How did they influence our decisions?

In meeting new faculty members, I have discovered that many teachers have a vague knowledge of the famous Dr. Fox experiments, a knowledge just blurry enough to produce skepticism about any attempt to identify and define teaching excellence. In that study, originally published in the 1970s, three researchers hired an actor to deliver a lecture to a group of educators. They instructed him to make his delivery highly expressive and entertaining but to offer little content in a talk riddled with logical confusions and repetitions. The experimenters gave their "professor" a fictional curriculum vitae, complete with a list of publications, and called him Dr. Fox. When they asked listeners to rate the lecture, the numbers appeared quite favorable, and one of the respondents even claimed to have read some of Dr. Fox's work.[4]

Many faculty members familiar with this experiment have concluded that student ratings are useless because lectures filled with junk can "seduce" students if the teacher is entertaining. But on closer examination, the original Dr. Fox study had one major flaw: it asked the wrong questions. Many of the questions simply asked if the actor did what he was instructed to do. For example, he had been told to display expressiveness and enthusiasm, and one of the survey questions then asked, "Did he seem interested in his subject?"[5] No wonder the ratings were so high. Not a single one of the eight questions asked the audience members if they had learned anything—the element we regarded as so crucial in spotting excellent teaching. Researchers made no effort to test the listeners on the knowledge they had gained from the lectures (although subsequent experiments with Dr. Fox did so), or even to ask them whether they believed they had in fact learned anything.

Far less well known and publicized were the subsequent studies done on what came to be known as the "Dr. Fox effect," which pointed out these methodological flaws in the original study and drew far more conservative conclusions from the investigations. All told, what we can learn about identifying teaching excellence from the Dr. Fox experiments seems pretty meager. At best, they may help us understand what questions we should and shouldn't be asking on the student rating forms. Rather than asking if professors were expressive or used a particular technique, we should ask if they helped students learn or stimulated their interest in the subject. Indeed, research has found high positive correlations between student ratings and external measures of student learning when such questions are used.[6] Most important, student ratings can, as one observer put it, "report the extent to which the students have been reached [educationally]."[7] If we want to know if students think that something has helped and encouraged them to learn, what better way to find out than to ask them. As for expressiveness, Herbert Marsh, an Australian researcher, and others found in subsequent Dr. Fox experiments that students usually perform better on examinations after hearing exciting lecturers than they do after dull ones, but that should surprise no one.[8]

Students do not always have sophisticated definitions of what it means to learn in a particular discipline. Thus we could not rely on the numbers alone to tell us whether someone had been helping people learn at the high level expected in this study. That information came only from looking at course materials, including syllabi and methods of evaluation, or from interviewing both instructors and their students. Student ratings could help supplement these more qualitative inquires, especially the numbers that emerge from questions like the two that appeared on both the Northwestern and the Vanderbilt student rating forms: Rate how much the teaching helped you learn, and rate how well the course stimulated you intellectually.

Yet many people remain highly suspicious of any study of teaching quality that draws even part of its evidence from student ratings. Educators not familiar with the Dr. Fox experiments may have a headline acquaintance with a more recent study. In 1993 Nalini Ambady and Robert Rosenthal showed students short film clips of teachers and asked them to rate those professors using the same instrument others had used after taking classes with the same instructors.[9] The researchers wanted to know how small the exposure could be and still generate ratings that were substantially the same as those that came after an entire semester of viewing the professor. When *Lingua Franca* and other publications reported that high positive correlations began to appear after the experimental group saw only a few seconds of the professor, some academics came to believe that all student ratings arise from superficial observations and amount to little more than the most primitive of popularity tests. These critics failed to consider, however, that the Ambady and Rosenthal study could point to a much different conclusion: students, with long histories of dealing with both highly stimulating and discouraging teachers, may develop an ability to guess quite accurately, even after only a few seconds of exposure, which professors will ultimately advance their education and which will not. In short, the instant judgments may stem from concerns about who can help them learn and grow rather than from a focus on amorphous qualities of personality and friendship. Ambady and Rosenthal made this point in their article: "Not only do we possess the remarkable ability to form impressions of others . . . but, perhaps more remarkably, the impressions that we form can be quite accurate!"

For our part, we have relied not on instant impressions but rather on the kind of detailed and sustained study outlined above and discussed more fully in the pages to come. I will return in the last chapter to the process of evaluating teaching, but for now it is worth emphasizing that this study follows the criteria of outcomes. We identify teaching excellence when we see evidence about remarkable feats of student learning and indications that the teaching helped and encouraged those results; we learn something about developing teaching excellence when we try to discover what fostered that educational success. Ratings from students of how much they learned and whether the professor stimulated their interests and intellectual development often told us a good deal about the quality of teaching, but we looked at far more evidence before concluding that it was exceptional.

MAJOR CONCLUSIONS

Let's begin with the major conclusions of this study, the broad patterns of thinking and practice we found among our subjects. One word of caution, however: anyone who expects a simple list of do's and don'ts may be greatly disappointed. The ideas here require careful and sophisticated thinking, deep professional learning, and often fundamental conceptual shifts. They do not lend themselves to teaching by the numbers.[10]

Our conclusions emerge from six broad questions we asked about the teachers we examined.

1. What Do the Best Teachers Know and Understand?

Without exception, outstanding teachers know their subjects extremely well. They are all active and accomplished scholars, artists, or scientists. Some have long and impressive publication lists, the kind the academy has long valued. Others have more modest records; or in a few cases, virtually none at all. But whether well published or not, the outstanding teachers follow the important intellectual and scientific or artistic developments within their fields, do research, have important and original thoughts on their subjects, study carefully and extensively what other people are doing in their fields, often read extensively in other fields (sometimes far distant from their own), and take a strong interest in the broader issues of their disciplines: the histories, controversies, and epistemological discussions. In short, they can do intellectually, physically, or emotionally what they expect from their students.

None of that should surprise anyone. This finding simply confirms that people are unlikely to become great teachers unless they know something to teach. The quality of knowing a discipline isn't particularly distinctive, however. If it were, every great scholar would be a great teacher. But that's not the case. More important, the people in our study, unlike so many others, have used their knowledge to develop techniques for grasping fundamental principles and organizing concepts that others can use to begin building their own understanding and abilities. They know how to simplify and clarify complex subjects, to cut to the heart of the matter with provocative insights, and they can think about their own thinking in the discipline, analyzing its nature and evaluating its quality. That capacity to think metacognitively drives much of what we observed in the best teaching.

We also found that our subjects have at least an intuitive understanding of human learning akin to the ideas that have been emerging from research in the learning sciences (see Chapter 2 for details).[11] They often use the same language, concepts, and ways of characterizing learning that we found in the literature. While others, for example, talk about transmitting knowledge and building a storehouse of information in the students' brains, our subjects talk about helping learners grapple with ideas and information to construct their understanding. Even their conception of what it means to learn in a particular course bears the mark of this distinction. While others might be satisfied if students perform well on the examinations, the best teachers assume that learning has little meaning unless it produces a sustained and substantial influence on the way people think, act, and feel.

2. How Do They Prepare to Teach?

Exceptional teachers treat their lectures, discussion sections, problem-based sessions, and other elements of teaching as serious intellectual endeavors as intellectually demanding and important as their research and scholarship. That attitude is probably most apparent in the answers our subjects gave to a simple question: "What do you ask yourself when you prepare to teach?" In some teachers that inquiry might have prompted uninspired responses that emphasized the mundane: How many students will I have? What will I include in my lectures? How many and what kind of tests will I give? What will I assign to read?

While those questions are important, they reflect a conception of teaching much different from the one embodied in the preparation of the people we studied. Our subjects use a much richer line of inquiry to design a class, lecture, discussion section, clerkship, or any other encounter with students, and they begin with questions about student learning objectives rather than about what the teacher will do. Chapter 3 examines the pattern of questions we heard most frequently and the conceptions of teaching and learning reflected in those inquiries.

3. What Do They Expect of Their Students?

Simply put, the best teachers expect "more." But given that many professors "pile it on" their classes without necessarily producing great learning results, what do the most successful teachers do to stimulate high achievement? The short answer is that they avoid objectives that are arbitrarily tied to the course and favor those that embody the kind of thinking and acting expected for life. Chapter 4 explores such practices and thinking more fully.

4. What Do They Do When They Teach?

While methods vary, the best teachers often try to create what we have come to call a "natural critical learning environment." In that environment, people learn by confronting intriguing, beautiful, or important problems, authentic tasks that will challenge them to grapple with ideas, rethink their assumptions, and examine their mental models of reality. These are challenging yet supportive conditions in which learners feel a sense of control over their education; work collaboratively with others; believe that their work will be considered fairly and honestly; and try, fail, and receive feedback from expert learners in advance of and separate from any summative judgment of their effort. In Chapter 5 I discuss in detail the various methods the best professors use to offer a lecture, conduct a discussion, teach a case, or create other learning opportunities that help build this environment.

5. How Do They Treat Students?

Highly effective teachers tend to reflect a strong trust in students. They usually believe that students want to learn, and they assume, until proven otherwise, that they can. They often display openness with students and may, from time to time, talk about their own intellectual journey, its ambitions, triumphs, frustrations, and failures, and encourage their students to be similarly reflective and candid. They may discuss how they developed their interests, the major obstacles they have faced in mastering the subject, or some of their secrets for learning particular material. They often discuss openly and enthusiastically their own sense of awe and curiosity about life. Above all, they tend to treat students with what can only be called simple decency.

6. How Do They Check Their Progress and Evaluate Their Efforts?

All the teachers we studied have some systematic program—some more elaborate than others—to assess their own efforts and to make appropriate changes. Furthermore, because they are checking their own efforts when they evaluate students, they avoid judging them on arbitrary standards. Rather, the assessment of students flows from primary learning objectives. In Chapter 7 I discuss some methods they use to collect feedback on their teaching, how they use evaluation of students to help accomplish that end, and how they design the grading to keep the focus on real learning objectives.

Three more general points need to be made before I move on: First, this is a book about what outstanding teachers do well; it's not intended to imply that they don't ever come up short or that they don't struggle to achieve good teaching. They all had to learn how to foster learning, and they must constantly remind themselves of what can go wrong, always reaching for new ways to understand what it means to learn and how best to foster that achievement. Even the best teachers have bad days, as they scramble to reach students. As the study revealed, they are not immune to frustrations, lapses in judgment, worry, or failure. They don't even always follow their own best practices. Nobody is perfect. As we move through the book, emphasizing what works best, it may be easy to forget those imperfections, or to think that great teachers are born, not made. Yet the evidence suggests otherwise. I suspect that part of the success they do enjoy stems, in part, from the willingness to confront their own weaknesses and failures. When we asked one of our earliest subjects, a philosophy professor from Vanderbilt, to give a public talk about his teaching, he tellingly chose as his title, "When my teaching fails."

Second, they didn't blame their students for any of the difficulties they faced. Some of our subjects taught only the best of students;

others, only the weakest; but many worked with individuals from a variety of backgrounds. We wanted to know what cut across all these grounds, whether anything was common to the best teaching in both highly selective institutions and schools with the most open of admissions policies.

Third, we noticed that the people we selected generally had a strong sense of commitment to the academic community and not just to personal success in the classroom. They saw their own efforts as a small part of a larger educational enterprise rather than as an opportunity to display personal prowess. In their minds, they were mere contributors to a learning environment that demanded attention from a fellowship of scholars. They frequently worked on major curricular initiatives and joined public conversations about how to improve teaching in the institution. Many of them talked about how the success of their own teaching hinged on something students learned in other classes. Consequently, they tended to maintain vigorous exchanges with colleagues about how best to educate students and often cited something they learned from working with others. Fundamentally, they were learners, constantly trying to improve their own efforts to foster students' development, and never completely satisfied with what they had already achieved.

LEARNING FROM THE STUDY

How can anyone use these conclusions to improve their teaching? The full answer to this simple question will take the entire book to explain, but an initial point seems obvious: We cannot take single pieces of the patterns noted here and simply combine them with other, less effective or even destructive habits and expect them to transform someone's teaching any more than adopting Rembrandt's brush strokes would, by itself, replicate his genius. We must understand the thinking, attitudes, values, and concepts that lie behind pedagogical masterpieces, observe practices carefully but then begin to digest, transform, and individualize what we see. To take the Rembrandt analogy a step further, the great Dutch artist could not be Picasso any more than the Spanish painter could replicate his predecessor; each had to find his own genius. So too must teachers adjust every idea to who they are and what they teach.

Ultimately, I hope this book will inspire readers to make a systematic and reflective appraisal of their own teaching approaches and strategies, asking themselves why they do certain kinds of things and not others. What evidence about how people learn drives their teaching choices? How often do they do something only because their professors did it? Ideally, readers will treat their teaching as they likely already treat their own scholarship or artistic creations: as serious and important intellectual and creative work, as an endeavor that benefits from careful observation and close analysis, from revision and refinement, and from dialogues with colleagues and the critiques of peers. Most of all, I hope readers will take away from this book the conviction that good teaching can be learned.

WHAT DO THEY KNOW ABOUT HOW WE LEARN?

In the early 1980s, two physicists at Arizona State University wanted to know whether a typical introductory physics course, with its traditional emphasis on Newton's laws of motion, changed the way students thought about motion. As you read this account, you might substitute for the line "think about motion" any other phrase that fits your subject. Do the students in any class change the way they think?

To find out, Ibrahim Abou Halloun and David Hestenes devised and validated an examination to determine how students understand motion. They gave the test to people entering the classes of four different physics professors, all good teachers according to both colleagues and their students. On the front side, the results surprised no one. Most students entered the course with an elementary, intuitive theory about the physical world, what the physicists called "a cross between Aristotelian and 14th-century impetus ideas." In short, they did not think about motion the way Isaac Newton did, let alone like Richard Feynman. But that was before the students took introductory physics.

Did the course change student thinking? Not really. After the term was over, the two physicists gave their examination once more and discovered that the course had made comparatively small changes in the way students thought.[1] Even many "A" students continued to think like Aristotle rather than like Newton. They had memorized formulae and learned to plug the right numbers into them, but they did not change their basic conceptions. Instead, they had interpreted everything they heard about motion in terms of the intuitive framework they had brought with them to the course.

Halloun and Hestenes wanted to probe this disturbing result a little further. They conducted individual interviews with some of the people who continued to reject Newton's perspectives to see if they could dissuade them from their misguided assumptions. During those interviews, they asked the students questions about some elementary motion problems, questions that required them to rely on their theories about motion to predict what would happen in a simple physics experiment. The students made their projections, and then the researchers performed the experiment in front of them so they could see whether they got it right. Obviously, those who relied on inadequate theories about motion had faulty predictions. At that point, the physicists asked the students to explain the discrepancy between their ideas and the experiment.

What they heard astonished them: many of the students still refused to give up their mistaken ideas about motion. Instead, they argued that the experiment they had just witnessed did not exactly apply to the law of motion in question; it was a special case, or it didn't quite fit the mistaken theory or law that they held as true. "As a rule," Halloun and Hestenes wrote, "students held firm to mistaken beliefs even when confronted with phenomena that contradicted those beliefs." If the researchers pointed out a contradiction or the students recognized one, "they tended at first not to question their own beliefs, but to argue that the observed instance was governed by some other law or principle and the principle they were using applied to a slightly different case."[2] The students performed all kinds of mental gymnastics to avoid confronting and revising the fundamental underlying principles that guided their understanding of the physical universe. Perhaps most disturbing, some of these students had received high grades in the class.

This story is part of a small but growing body of literature that

questions whether students always learn as much as we have traditionally thought they did. The scholarly work on this issue asks not
if students can pass our examinations but whether their education
has a sustained, substantial, and positive influence on the way they
think, act, and feel. Researchers have found that even some "good"
students may not progress as much intellectually as we once
thought. They have discovered that some people make A's by learning to "plug and chug," memorizing formulae, sticking numbers in
the right equation or the right vocabulary into a paper, but understanding little. When the class is over, they quickly forget much of
what they have "learned."[3] Participants at a 1987 conference on science education, for example, saw this problem in math. "Those
who successfully complete calculus," they concluded, "frequently
fail to gain a conceptual understanding of the subject or an appreciation of its importance" because instructors rely on "'plug and
chug' exercises that have little connection with the real world."[4]
Even when learners have acquired some conceptual understanding
of a discipline or field, they are often unable to link that knowledge
to real-world situations or problem-solving contexts.

LEARNING FROM THE BEST

What do the best teachers know that helps them overcome—at least
partially and sometimes fully—these problems?

We discovered that they know their disciplines well and are
active and accomplished scholars, artists, or scientists—even if they
do not always have long publication records. But that necessary
knowledge alone can't account for their teaching success. If it did,
then any expert in the field would become an outstanding educator,
but that clearly doesn't happen. Nor is it the case that experts just
need more time to become better teachers. We encountered many
professors, all eminent scholars in their fields, who spent hours

crafting lectures that reflected the latest and most advanced scholarly and scientific knowledge only to produce students who understood little of that sophistication. One of those people, a medical school professor who was not part of the study, once told us with both pride and some measure of frustration that he didn't worry about whether students "got it" as long as every line of his lectures reflected the "highest standards of scientific quality and cutting-edge knowledge in the field."

What else do the best teachers know that might explain their successes in helping students learn deeply? We found two other kinds of knowledge that seem to be at play. First, they have an unusually keen sense of the histories of their disciplines, including the controversies that have swirled within them, and that understanding seems to help them reflect deeply on the nature of thinking within their fields. They can then use that ability to think about their own thinking—what we call "metacognition"—and their understanding of the discipline qua discipline to grasp how other people might learn. They know what has to come first, and they can distinguish between foundational concepts and elaborations or illustrations of those ideas. They realize where people are likely to face difficulties developing their own comprehension, and they can use that understanding to simplify and clarify complex topics for others, tell the right story, or raise a powerfully provocative question. There's a catch to all this, however. That kind of understanding is obviously rooted in each individual field of study and defies generalization.

Yet something else seems to be at work that transcends the various disciplines and therefore is more useful to our general study. To put it simply, the people we analyzed have generally cobbled together from their own experiences working with students conceptions of human learning that are remarkably similar to some ideas that have emerged in the research and theoretical literature on cognition, motivation, and human development. Those ideas help them understand and cope with situations like the physics story and myriad other learning problems.

Here are the key concepts we found.

1. Knowledge Is Constructed, Not Received

Perhaps the best way to understand this notion is to contrast it with an older idea. According to the traditional view, memory is a great storage bin. We put knowledge in it and then later pick out what we need. Thus you often hear people say, "My students must learn the material before they can think about it," presumably meaning that they must store it somewhere for later use.

The best teachers don't think of memory that way, and neither do a lot of learning scientists. Instead, they say that we construct our sense of reality out of all the sensory input we receive, and that process begins in the crib. We see, hear, feel, smell, and taste, and we begin connecting all those sensations in our brains to build patterns of the way we think the world works. So our brains are both storage and processing units. At some point, we begin using those existing patterns to understand new sensory input. By the time we reach college, we have thousands of mental models, or schemas, that we use to try to understand the lectures we hear, the texts we read, and so forth.

For example, I have a mental model of something called a classroom. When I enter a room and receive some sensory input through the lens in my eyes, I understand the input in terms of that previously existing model, and I know I'm not in a train station. But this enormously useful ability can also present problems for learners. When we encounter new material, we try to comprehend it in terms of something we think we already know. We use our existing mental models to shape the sensory inputs we receive. That means that when we talk to students, our thoughts do not travel seamlessly from our brains to theirs. The students bring paradigms to the class that shape how they construct meaning. Even if they know nothing about our subjects, they still use an existing mental model of something to build their knowledge of what we tell them, often leading to an understanding that is quite different from what we intend to convey. "The trouble with people," Josh Billings once remarked, "is not that they don't know but that they know so much that ain't so!"

I'm not just saying that students bring misconceptions to class, as a philosophy professor concluded a few years ago when he heard these ideas in a workshop. Actually, I'm arguing something much more fundamental: the teachers we encountered believe everybody constructs knowledge and that we all use existing constructions to understand any new sensory input. When these highly effective educators try to teach the basic facts in their disciplines, they want students to see a portion of reality the way the latest research and scholarship in the discipline has come to see it. They don't think of it as just getting students to "absorb some knowledge," as many other people put it. Because they believe that students must use their existing mental models to interpret what they encounter, they think about what they do as stimulating construction, not "transmitting knowledge." Furthermore, because they recognize that the higher-order concepts of their disciplines often run counter to the models of reality that everyday experience has encouraged most people to construct, they often want students to do something that human beings don't do very well: build new mental models of reality.

But that's the problem.

2. Mental Models Change Slowly

How can we stimulate students to build new models, to engage in what some call "deep" learning as opposed to "surface" learning in which they merely remember something long enough to pass the examination? Our subjects generally believe that to accomplish that feat, learners must (1) face a situation in which their mental model will not work (that is, will not help them explain or do something); (2) care that it does not work strongly enough to stop and grapple with the issue at hand; and (3) be able to handle the emotional trauma that sometimes accompanies challenges to longstanding beliefs.

The teachers in our study often talked about "challenging students intellectually." That meant they wanted to create what some of the literature calls an "expectation failure," a situation in which existing mental models will lead to faulty expectations, causing their students to realize the problems they face in believing whatever they believe. Yet these highly effective teachers realized that human beings face too many expectation failures in life to care about all of them, so students may not engage in the deep thinking required to build completely new models. Furthermore, they understood that people have so many paradigms of reality that they may not know which of their schemas has led to the faulty predictions, so they may correct the wrong ones. That's partly where the physics students went wrong when they encountered experiments in which their conceptions of motion did not work. Finally, the best teachers understood that their students may find so much emotional comfort in some existing model of reality that they cling to it even in the face of repeated expectation failures.

Such ideas have important implications for the teachers. They conduct class and craft assignments in a way that allows students to try their own thinking, come up short, receive feedback, and try again. They give students a safe space in which to construct ideas, and they often spend a great deal of time creating a kind of scaffolding to help students engage in that construction (which is different from the popular notion of "covering" the material, but in ways that are sometimes difficult to grasp). Because they attempt to place students in situations in which some of their mental models will not work, they try to understand those models and the emotional baggage attached to them. They listen to student conceptions before challenging them. Rather than telling students they are wrong and then providing the "correct" answers, they often ask questions to help students see their own mistakes.

Perhaps this general approach is most apparent in the way the teachers in the study approached a controversy that still rages in many disciplines, from the sciences to the humanities. On one side of that debate, teachers have argued that students cannot learn to think, to analyze, to synthesize, and to make judgments until they "know" the "basic facts" of the discipline. People in this school of thought have tended to emphasize the delivery of information to the exclusion of all other teaching activities. They seldom expect their students to reason (that will supposedly come after they have "learned the material"). On their examinations, these professors often test for recall, or simple recognition of information (on a multiple-choice examination, for example).

Teachers in our study come down on the other side of that controversy. They believe that students must learn the facts *while* learning to use them to make decisions about what they understand or what they should do. To them, "learning" makes little sense unless it has some sustained influence on the way the learner subsequently thinks, acts, or feels. So they teach the "facts" in a rich context of problems, issues, and questions.

Consider the approaches of two anatomy professors, one who has been enormously successful and was included in the study and the other, outside the study, who has, to put it gently, had difficulty fostering learning. The latter insisted that students must simply "learn the facts." There "isn't much to discuss," he told us. "The structure of the human body is well known by scientists, and students must simply absorb a lot of facts. There isn't any other way to teach except to stand in front of them and give them those facts. We can't discuss the way you might in a literature class." He talked about "transmitting" knowledge and insisted that the primary objective of the course was to "memorize large chunks of information."

The students must, he said, "commit it all to memory, store it away." His examinations reflected the same line of thinking. They required students largely to reproduce what the professor told them in class or to recognize correct answers. When we talked with some of his students, they often confessed that they had difficulty recalling information several months after the course was over. Meanwhile, the professor complained to us that students generally "didn't study hard enough" and that the "weak students" simply had difficulty "holding very much in their memory banks."

The other professor talked not about "absorbing information" but about "understanding" structures, how individual parts related to the whole, and—most important—the kinds of decisions that students would be able to make with the comprehension they "developed." She talked about helping students "build" their understanding and learn to "use the information" to solve problems, both scientific and medical. In class, she often did explain "how things work," trying to "simplify and clarify" basic concepts and ideas, but she also introduced problems, often clinical cases of "what could go wrong," and engaged the students in grappling with the issues those examples raised. Students encountered the information in the context of struggling, first with understanding and then with application of that comprehension. "I have to think," she told us, "about why anyone would want to remember particular pieces of information. What does this fact help you understand? What problems does it help you address?" She consciously thought about the "faulty paradigms" that the students brought with them to the class and crafted her explanations, discussions, and reading materials to challenge those notions. Her examinations followed suit. They asked students to struggle with clinical cases, to develop and defend their analyses, syntheses, and evaluations of those cases. They still had to recall a large body of information, but they also had to reason through problems.

3. Questions Are Crucial

In the learning literature and in the thinking of the best teachers, questions play an essential role in the process of learning and modifying mental models. Questions help us construct knowledge. They point to holes in our memory structures and are critical for indexing the information that we attain when we develop an answer for that inquiry. Some cognitive scientists think that questions are so important that we cannot learn until the right one has been asked: if memory does not ask the question, it will not know where to index the answer. The more questions we ask, the more ways we can index a thought in memory. Better indexing produces greater flexibility, easier recall, and richer understanding.

"When we can successfully stimulate our students to ask their own questions, we are laying the foundation for learning," one professor told us in a theme we heard repeatedly. "We define the questions that our course will help them to answer," another reminded us, "but we want them, along the way, to develop their own set of rich and important questions about our discipline and our subject matter."

4. Caring Is Crucial

People learn best when they ask an important question that they care about answering, or adopt a goal that they want to reach. If they don't care, they will not try to reconcile, explain, modify, or integrate new knowledge with old. They will not try to construct new mental models of reality. They may remember information for a short period (long enough to take the test), but only when their memory generates questions will it be prepared to change knowledge structures. Only then does it know where to place something. If we are not seeking an answer to anything, we pay little attention to random information.

These ideas about learning can help explain the story I told at the beginning of this chapter. Those physics students who made A's yet failed to grasp anything about Newtonian concepts had not rebuilt their mental models about motion. They had merely learned to plug numbers into formulae without experiencing an expectation failure with the universes they imagined in their minds. They took all they heard from their professors and simply wrapped it around some pre-existing model of how motion works. Perhaps because they were focused on grades rather than on understanding the physical universe, they didn't care enough to grapple with their own ideas and build new paradigms of reality.

So what do the best teachers understand about motivation that enables them to help students care?

WHAT MOTIVATES? WHAT DISCOURAGES?

We found that highly successful teachers have developed a series of attitudes, conceptions, and practices that reflected well some key insights that have emerged from the scholarship on motivation.

For the last forty years or more, psychologists have studied what would happen if someone had a strong interest in doing something, and someone else offered them an "extrinsic" reward to bolster their "intrinsic" interest and then later withdrew that reinforcement. Would their fascination go up, stay the same, or go down? If, for example, students have a strong curiosity about what causes wars and we offer them extrinsic rewards in the form of grades to motivate their learning and then they later graduate, what will happen to their interests?

They actually go down. Research subjects tend to lose some or all of their intrinsic fascination once the extrinsic motivator is gone, at least under certain conditions. In one famous series of experiments, Edward L. Deci and his colleagues had two groups of students play with a block-construction puzzle called *Soma*. The subjects were brought to an examination room and asked to solve the puzzle. Each time the examiner would leave the room for eight minutes. The psychologists wanted to know whether and how long the subjects would play with the *Soma* while they were gone (they observed the students from behind a one-way glass).

One group of subjects never got any rewards for solving the puzzle and never lost interest. A second group received money part of the time and lost interest when the compensation ended. Deci and others have performed scores of such experiments, trying several arrangements to see what would happen; they have consistently found that most extrinsic motivators damage intrinsic motivation. They have also found that if they use "verbal reinforcement and positive feedback"—in other words, encouragement or praise— they can stimulate interest, or at least keep it from evaporating.[5]

How do we account for the differences, and what do those differences tell us about motivating students to learn? Deci, Richard deCharms, and others have theorized that people lose much of their motivation if they think they are being manipulated by the external reward, if they lose what the psychologists have called their sense of the "locus of causality" of their behavior.[6] In other words, if people see certain conduct as a way to get a particular reward or avoid a punishment, then they will engage in those activities only when "they want the rewards and when they believe the rewards will be forthcoming from the behavior."[7] If they do not want that particular payoff, or if the possibility of reward is subsequently removed, they will lose interest in that activity. By contrast, as Deci put it, "verbal reinforcement, social approval, and so on . . . are less likely to be perceived by the person as controlling" behavior.[8] The key seems to be how the subject views the reward.

Investigators have also found that performance—not just motivation—can decrease when subjects believe that other people are trying to control them. If students study only because they want to get a good grade or be the best in the class, they do not achieve as much as they do when they learn because they are interested. They will not solve problems as effectively, they will not analyze as well, they will not synthesize with the same mental skill, they will not reason as logically, nor will they ordinarily even take on the same kinds of challenges. They will usually opt for easier problems while those who work from intrinsic motivations will pick more ambitious tasks. They may become what some literature calls "strategic learners," focusing primarily on doing well in school, avoiding any challenges that will harm their academic performance and record, and often failing to develop deep understandings. Moreover, the effects seem to last. If students have been offered tangible extrinsic rewards to solve problems successfully and later lose those stimuli, they will continue to use less logical and efficient procedures than will students who never had the external incentive.[9]

Even certain kinds of verbal praise can be detrimental to learning. Young children who constantly hear "person" praise ("you're so smart to do this well") as opposed to "task" praise ("you did that well") are more likely to believe that intelligence is fixed rather than expandable with hard work. When they subsequently face setbacks after receiving person praise, their views of intelligence can cause them to develop a sense of helplessness ("I'm not as smart as I once thought I was"). When researchers asked these children to describe what made them feel smart, they talked about tasks they found easy, that required little effort, and that they could do before anyone else without making mistakes. In contrast, their peers who thought they got smarter by trying harder and learning new things said they felt intelligent when they didn't understand something, tried really hard, and then got it, or figured out something new. In other words, the children with the fixed view of intelligence and a sense of helplessness felt smart only when they avoided those activities most likely to help them learn—struggling, grappling, and making mistakes.[10]

These children are likely to have "performance goals." They want to achieve perfection or get the "right" answer to impress other people because they want to appear to be one of the "smart people." They are afraid of making mistakes. They will often carefully calculate how much they need to achieve to win the proper praise and do no more than that, for fear that they might fail in the eyes of others. Some of these people do excel by some standards, but they still achieve primarily for the sake of that external recognition and fall short of where they might go. In contrast, students who believe that they can become more intelligent by learning (a "mastery orientation") often work essentially to increase their own competence (adopting "learning goals"), not to win rewards.[11] They are more likely to take risks in learning, to try harder tasks, and consequently learn more than children who are performance-oriented.[12]

What implications do these findings have for an academic culture that uses grades as a system of rewards and punishments? Is there a way to use grades that will not cause students to feel like they are being manipulated by the evaluation process? How can we best respond to students who develop a sense of helplessness? What do the best teachers do to keep students from becoming grade-grubbers and to stimulate an intrinsic interest in the subject?

In general, the people we investigated tried to avoid extrinsic motivators and to foster intrinsic ones, moving students toward learning goals and a mastery orientation. They gave students as much control over their own education as possible and displayed both a strong interest in their learning and a faith in their abilities. They offered nonjudgmental feedback on students' work, stressed opportunities to improve, constantly looked for ways to stimulate advancement, and avoided dividing their students into the sheep and the goats. Rather than pitting people against each other, they encouraged cooperation and collaboration. In general, they avoided grading on the curve, and instead gave everyone the opportunity to achieve the highest standard and grades.

Many of the best teachers do what Jeanette Norden does in her medical school classes: grade students on the knowledge and abilities they have developed by the end of the class rather than on an average of accomplishments displayed throughout the term. For Norden and others, that means making each examination comprehensive, giving students multiple chances to demonstrate their comprehension. It also means constructing examinations with the greatest care to test the appropriate abilities comprehensively.

This practice of giving students many chances to demonstrate their learning parallels elements that Richard Light found in his study of the most intellectually satisfying classes at Harvard. Light and his colleagues interviewed thousands of current and former students, asking them about the qualities of the best courses they had taken at the university. In his 1990 initial report of findings, Light noticed that the "characteristics of highly respected courses" included "high demands" but "with plentiful opportunities to revise and improve their work before it receives a grade, thereby learning from their mistakes in the process."[13]

Most important, our outstanding teachers generally avoided using grades to persuade students to study. Instead, they invoked the subject, the questions it raises, and the promises it makes to any learner. In doing so, they displayed their own enthusiasm for the issues contained in the material. "I believe that if you've chosen your field properly," explained a professor of Slavic languages and literatures, "you've chosen it because it answers what I call the god inside of you—or if you like, the devil inside of you. If the students see you pursuing that, with all your heart, all your soul, and all your might, they'll respond."

This approach is apparent in a thousand little practices but probably most evident in the routine many outstanding teachers follow the first day of class. Rather than laying out a set of requirements for students, they usually talk about the promises of the course, about the kinds of questions the discipline will help students answer, or about the intellectual, emotional, or physical abilities that it will help them develop. To be sure, they also explain what students will be doing to realize those promises—what many of us call the requirements—but they avoid the language of demands and use the vocabulary of promises instead. They invite, rather than command, and often display the attributes of someone inviting colleagues to dinner rather than the demeanor of a bailiff summoning someone to court.

The business of giving students some sense of control over their own education is no mean feat given that professors control both the curriculum and the questions that arise within each course. But our subjects managed to do it primarily by helping students see the connection between the questions of the course and the questions that students might bring to that course. Consider, for example, how we come to the questions and issues that currently drive our lives as scientists and scholars. Questions that interest us are usually important because of some previous inquiry, which, in turn, was significant because of some earlier question, which derived its own importance from some still earlier investigation, and so forth. We often live our scholarly lives focused on matters that lie several layers beneath the surface of topics that first intrigued us.

We saw teachers who dig back toward the surface, meet their students there, recapture the significance of those inquiries, and help people to understand why this question fascinates anyone. They do not simply call out from their position deep within the ground and ask students to join their subterranean mining expeditions. They help students to understand the connection between current topics and some larger and more fundamental inquiry, and in so doing find common ground in those "big questions" that first motivated their own efforts to learn. "How could you not be interested in organic chemistry?" David Tuleen asked. "It is the very basis of life itself."

A twentieth-century U.S. diplomatic history course, for example, usually spends some time on events immediately after World War I:

Woodrow Wilson's trip to Versailles, his attempt to win passage of the treaty and acceptance of U.S. entry into the League of Nations, his failure to take Republican leaders to France with him, his conflicts with Henry Cabot Lodge, and the divisions existing in the Senate at the time of the League vote, among others. It's a compelling story that Hollywood has used at least twice in popular movies. It even contains some elements of classic tragedy—Wilson orders supporters to vote against the treaty rather than accept a compromise. Yet students' interests in these topics always seem to hinge on whether they become intrigued with the personal story of Woodrow Wilson. If they do, bingo, you have them. If not, you lose them. Without that interest, some students have no concern for any of the scholarship surrounding this history. Who cares? they say.

Who does care, and why? Why do historians study these events? Not simply because they happened—many events happen that never attract the attention of scholars. If you trace the original scholarly interest in Wilson's trip to Paris (at least the interest that first appeared during World War II) you will find it emerged from a simple, yet important, series of higher questions: Could Wilson, or any other powerful individual, have prevented World War II with a different course of action in 1919 and 1920? Can human beings avoid wars? Furthermore, behind these questions lies an even more fundamental inquiry: Can people control their own destiny, or does some kind of determinism, economic or otherwise, sweep us along, making us hapless observers and chroniclers of our own fate and the antics of even a powerful individual such as Woodrow Wilson insignificant? These are big questions that intrigue and provoke virtually all students. It was this level of question that we often saw in the classes we studied, and it was an appeal to this kind of inquiry rather than to extrinsic motivators that captivated students.

The most effective teachers help students keep the larger questions of the course constantly at the forefront. Donald Saari, a mathematician from the University of California, invokes the principle of what he calls "WGAD"—"Who gives a damn?" At the beginning of his courses, he tells his students that they are free to ask him this question on any day during the course, at any moment in class. He will stop and explain to his students why the material under consideration at that moment—however abstruse and minuscule a piece of the big picture it may be—is important, and how it relates to the larger questions and issues of the course.

Nancy MacLean, Charles Deering McCormick Professor of Teaching Excellence and Professor of History at Northwestern, offered these details: "On the first day of all my courses . . . I devote some time to the promised 'payoff,' connecting course themes or required skills to issues or interest likely to be on their minds. Some people might find this crude; I don't. Or rather, I don't care if it is: we're all too busy these days to show interest in something if we can't see why it might matter." As an example of how she does this, she mentioned a woman's history course she recently taught, during which her students informed her about a book called *The Rules: Time-Tested Secrets for Capturing the Hearts of Mr. Right.* Surprised at the number of students familiar with this text—an informal poll showed 85 percent—she read it, inserted sections from it into the syllabus, and allowed students an option to write a paper about it, one that would "provide a historical analysis of this document, drawing on as many course materials as possible, that situated and made sense of it in historical context." MacLean's willingness to bend the syllabus to accommodate this text speaks volumes about her intuitive understanding of motivation: she helped students re-see a familiar object in light of the analytic and historical tools with which her course had equipped them. She built a solid connection between her questions and her students' lives and interests.

The people we explored know the value that intellectual challenges—even inducing puzzlement and confusion—can play in stimulating interest in the questions of their courses. Several of them talked about finding the novel, the incongruous, and the paradoxical. With carefully chosen analogies they make even the familiar seem strange and intriguing and the strange appear familiar. We found people who constantly sprinkle their classes with personal anecdotes and even emotional stories to illustrate otherwise purely intellectual topics and procedures. Many of them spoke about beginning with what seemed most familiar and fascinating to students and then weaving the new and different into the fabric of the course. One professor explained it this way: "It's sort of Socratic . . . You begin with a puzzle—you get somebody puzzled, and tied in knots, and mixed up." Those puzzles and knots generate questions for students, he went on to say, and then you begin to help them untie the knots.

In the broad literature on human motivation, there are frequent discussions of three factors that can influence different people in varied ways. Some people respond primarily to the challenge of mastering something, getting inside a subject and trying to understand it in all its complexity. Such people are considered deep learners. Others react well to competition, to the quest for the gold and the chance to do better than anyone else. While that can be a strong motivation for some, it can sometimes hinder learning. In the classroom, such individuals frequently become strategic learners, interested in making the high grades but seldom willing to grapple deeply enough to change their own perceptions. They learn for the test and then quickly expunge the material to make room for something else. "They are," Craig Nelson, a biology professor from Indiana, noted, "bulimic learners." Finally, we encounter people who seek primarily to avoid failure, what the literature calls "performance-avoiders." In the classroom, they often become surface learners, never willing to invest enough of themselves to probe a topic deeply because they fear failure, so they stick with trying to cope, to survive. They often resort to memorizing and trying simply to reproduce what they hear.

In interview after interview, we found professors who had a

strong sense of these categories of learners and a recognition that, if they tailored their appeals to individuals, they could influence how their students approached learning. They realized that human beings can and do change, and that the nature of their instruction can have an enormous influence on that process. "Performance avoiders" suffered from lack of self-confidence, so motivation to learn might come from a stronger belief that they can learn. The best teachers carefully constructed learning tasks and objectives to build confidence and to encourage, yet to give students strong challenges and a sense of sufficient accomplishment. They recognized also that the culture of some classrooms fosters bulimic learners, encouraging students to stress the regurgitation of facts and the subsequent purging.

"Schooling," one professor told us, "encourages many bright students to think of the enterprise as a competition to be won." Robert de Beaugrande said it just recently: "'Bulimic education' force-feeds the learner with a feast of 'facts' which are to be memorised and used for certain narrowly defined tasks, each leading to a single 'right answer' already decided by teacher or textbook. After this use, the facts are 'purged' to make room for the next feeding. 'Bulimic education' thus enforces an intensely local or short-range focus, irrespective of any long-range benefits that might arise from the succession of feed-purge cycles."[14]

To avoid such cycles, the teachers we observed usually abstain from appeals to competition. They stress the beauty, utility, or intrigue of the questions they try to answer with their students, and they pursue answers to questions rather than simply the "learning of information." They make promises to their students and try to help each one achieve as much as possible. Most important, they expect more than bulimic learning, crafting and outlining for their students fascinating notions about what it means to develop as intelligent and educated people. They bring to the table challenging objectives, but they also listen to their learners, to their ambitions, and try to help them understand those aspirations in more sophisticated and satisfying ways. "I often have students," one professor told us, "who do not yet realize the potential they have for learning and the unique contributions they can make." In Chapter 4, we will explore more fully how highly effective professors expect more and inspire their students to achieve it.

TAKING A DEVELOPMENTAL VIEW OF LEARNING

Finally, our subjects realized that learning doesn't just affect what you know; it can transform how you understand the nature of knowing. Many of the teachers were aware of the work that William Perry and a group of psychologists at Wellesley College have done to understand the intellectual development of undergraduates. Both Perry and Blythe McVicker Clinchy and her colleagues have suggested four broad categories through which students can eventually travel, each one with its concept of what it means to learn. At the most elementary level, students think that learning is simply a matter of checking with the experts, getting the "right answers," then memorizing them.[15] Clinchy called these people "received knowers." "Truth, for the received knower," she argued, is external. "She can ingest it, but she cannot evaluate it or create it for herself. The received knowers are the students who sit there, pencils poised, ready to write down every word the teacher says."[16] They expect education to operate on what Paulo Freire has dubbed the "banking model," in which teachers deposit the correct answers into students' heads.

Eventually, many students find out that experts disagree. As a result, they come to believe—in the second developmental stage— that all knowledge is a matter of opinion. These "subjective knowers" use feelings to make judgments: To them, "an idea is right if it feels right," as Clinchy puts it.[17] It is all a matter of opinion. If they receive low grades, students at this level will often say of the teacher, "she didn't like my opinion."

A few students eventually become "procedural knowers": they learn to "play the game" of the discipline. They recognize that it has criteria for making judgments and they learn how to use those standards in writing their papers. We usually recognize them as our sharpest students. Such "knowing" does not, however, influence how they think outside of class. They simply give the teacher what she wants without much sustained or substantial influence on the way they think, act, or feel.

Only at the highest level (what Perry calls "Commitment") do students become independent, critical, and creative thinkers, valuing the ideas and ways of thinking to which they are exposed and consciously and consistently trying to use them. They become aware of their own thinking and learn to correct it as they go. Clinchy and her colleagues found two types of knowers at the highest levels: "separate knowers" like to detach themselves from an idea, remaining objective, even skeptical, and always willing to argue about it. In contrast, "connected knowers" look at the merits of other people's ideas instead of trying to shoot them down. They are not "dispassionate, unbiased observers," the Wellesley study concluded. "They deliberately bias themselves in favor of the thing they are examining."[18]

According to this scheme, people don't just march upward; they move back and forth between levels and can operate on more than one developmental stage at a time. In their major they might rise to the level of procedural knowing; in other fields, they might remain received or subjective knowers. We might hear them demand "right answers" they can memorize, or watch them fail to make the distinctions our disciplines encourage and, therefore, think that all views are equally valid.

The best teachers talked about stimulating an "incremental

series" of changes in people's view of knowledge, and the need to adopt different approaches for various levels of learners. For received knowers, who often have trouble identifying relevant facts, they would encourage precise thinking (What are the key facts? What are the key definitions?). They confronted subjective knowing with the challenges of evidence and reason (How do we know this? Why do we accept or believe this idea?). For everyone, they taught the uncertainty of knowledge (What did scholars believe about this subject ten years ago? What are the questions we still need to answer?). For those students who have begun to master procedural knowing and are flirting with commitments, they would ask about their values and about the implications of their conclusions. But rather than rationing out such experiences in some planned lockstep, they tended to give all students all these experiences and challenges repeatedly, as if to recognize that while the process of maturing intellectually may involve incremental challenges, it is seldom linear. People develop in fits and starts and benefit from repeated challenges from a variety of levels. "Not every student benefits from the same set of experiences at the same time," concluded one professor, "and that's the reason I try to give different people different kinds of challenges. Students operate on different levels and will not all catch on at the same time."

Some instructors have deliberately introduced students to the concepts of connected and separate knowing and have acknowledged the value of both tendencies. They often tell their students that though they usually want them to be separate knowers, to be skeptical and adversarial, sometimes they want them to be connected knowers, to suspend judgment until they have a better understanding of something. Clinchy argues that while both men and women can be predominantly separate or connected knowers, more women than men prefer the latter. Thus she concluded that "educational practices based on an adversarial model may be more appropriate—or at least less stressful—for men than for women."[19] Yet among the professors in our study who were aware of these concepts, there was no clear pattern of either acceptance or rejection. Even so, the best teachers exhibited a special sensitivity both to the problems that all students face in navigating these sometimes treacherous and often disturbing waters and to the special problems that some encounter. They didn't say simply "if some students can learn" in a certain way, "all students can do so." Rather, they accommodated the diversity they found, and even responded with sympathy and understanding to the emotional transitions people undergo when they encounter new ideas and material. They recognized that students may experience feelings of resentment and hostility when they discover that truth does not reside in the heads of their teachers. They were familiar with the stages of intellectual transition and so understood when students responded strongly and viscerally to ideas and questions professors take for granted.

The most successful teachers expect the highest levels of development from their students. They reject the view of teaching as nothing more than delivering correct answers to students and learning as simply remembering those deliveries. They expect their students to rise above the category of received knowers, something they reflect in the way they teach and assess their students. They even draw clear distinctions between those students who "do the discipline" for the sake of the class (the procedural knowers) and those students whose ways of thinking and drawing conclusions are permanently transformed.

Whereas some professors might see their job as teaching the facts, concepts, and procedures of their subject, the teachers we studied emphasized the pursuit of answers to important questions and often encouraged students to use the methodologies, assumptions, and concepts from a variety of fields to solve complex problems. They often incorporated literature from other fields into their teaching and emphasized what it means to get an education. They spoke about the value of an integrated education rather than one fragmented between individual courses.

That is not to say that they did not teach their own disciplines. They did, but in the context of focusing on the intellectual, and often ethical, emotional, and artistic, development of their students. Indeed, rather than thinking just in terms of teaching history, biology, chemistry, or other topics, they talked about teaching *students* to understand, apply, analyze, synthesize, and evaluate evidence and conclusions. They stressed the ability to make judgments, to weigh evidence, and to think about one's own thinking. Many of them spoke about the importance of developing intellectual habits, of asking the right questions, of examining one's values, of aesthetic tastes, of recognizing moral decision, and of looking at the world in a different way. "I want my students to understand what we think we know in this field," one scientist explained, "but I also hope they will understand how we reached those conclusions and how those findings are subject to ongoing inquiry. I want them to ask, 'why do we think this is the case, what assumptions have we made, what evidence do we have, how have we reasoned to get to this point?' But I also want them to ask themselves about the implications our conclusions might have." Rather than emphasizing how well students could perform on examinations, they often talked about ways to transform conceptual understanding, foster advanced reasoning skills, and the ability to examine one's own thinking critically.

IMPLICATIONS FOR TEACHING

The major ideas that animate the best teachers stem from a very basic observation: Human beings are curious animals. People learn naturally while trying to solve problems that concern them. They develop an intrinsic interest that guides their quest for knowledge, and an intrinsic interest—and here's the rub—that can diminish in the face of extrinsic rewards and punishments that appear to manipulate their focus. People are most likely to enjoy their education if they believe they are in charge of the decision to learn.

The best college and university teachers create what we might call a natural critical learning environment in which they embed the skills and information they wish to teach in assignments (questions and tasks) students will find fascinating—authentic tasks that will arouse curiosity, challenging students to rethink their assumptions and examine their mental models of reality. They create a safe environment in which students can try, come up short, receive feedback, and try again. Students understand and remember what they have learned because they master and use the reasoning abilities necessary to integrate it with larger concepts. They become aware of the implications and applications of the ideas and information. They recognize the importance of measuring their own work intellectually as they do it, and in the process they routinely apply the intellectual standards of a variety of disciplines. They cease to be Aristotelian physicists and become Newtonian ones because they've come to care enough to question themselves.

HOW DO THEY PREPARE
TO TEACH?

Think for a moment about the kinds of questions you ask yourself when you prepare to teach. When I was a twenty-three-year-old rookie getting ready to conduct my first college course (a survey of United States history through the Civil War), I scribbled four questions on the back of an envelope. Years later I found that scrap of my youthful self tucked in an old notebook and discovered that my needs were apparently simple: Where's the classroom? What textbook will I use? What will I include in my lectures? How many tests will I give?

As we began our study, we played a game with the teachers: If college courses didn't exist and you wanted to invent them, what questions would you ask yourself? Their lists of inquiries were much richer than mine and remarkably similar to each other, regardless of discipline. As we probed this result we realized, however, that they were not simply reciting some litany of good practice they had memorized. Instead, the similarities stemmed from a deeper base, from primary conceptions of what it means to teach and learn that then shaped the way they prepared any learning experience. Like a flower that reflects the genetic code of its seed, their questions sprang from those fundamental ideas. If we want to benefit from their insights, we must understand both the flowers and that code.

At the core of most professors' ideas about teaching is a focus on what the teacher does rather than on what the students are supposed to learn. In that standard conception, teaching is something that instructors do to students, usually by delivering truths about the discipline. It is what some writers call a "transmission model." I must have held that view in 1965 because the limit of my questions made sense only from that perspective.

In contrast, the best educators thought of teaching as anything they might do to help and encourage students to learn. Teaching is engaging students, engineering an environment in which they learn. Equally important, they thought of the creation of that successful learning environment as an important and serious intellectual (or artistic) act, perhaps even as a kind of scholarship, that required the attention of the best minds in academia.[1] For our subjects, that scholarship centered around four fundamental inquiries: (1) What should my students be able to do intellectually, physically, or emotionally as a result of their learning? (2) How can I best help and encourage them to develop those abilities and the habits of the heart and mind to use them? (3) How can my students and I best understand the nature, quality, and progress of their learning? and (4) How can I evaluate my efforts to foster that learning?

Already we can begin to see a rich set of concerns. The first question draws on important thinking about the nature of a discipline or art form. It is a kind of epistemological investigation into what it means to know something, pushing far beyond the vague little phrases that often litter discussions of learning objectives ("learning the material," "thinking critically," "engaging the subject matter," "feeling comfortable with the topic," "taking it to a higher level"). In an attempt to define what such traditional language might mean, highly effective teachers often talk about what they want students to "do" intellectually rather than about what they should "learn." The other questions, however, survey matters that most disciplines do not study, and so depend on the vast and growing body of learning research and theory.

These two powerful notions—that teaching is fostering learning and that it requires serious intellectual work—appear quite clearly in a baker's dozen of specific planning questions we heard most often.

1. What big questions will my course help students answer, or what skills, abilities, or qualities will it help them develop, and how will I encourage my students' interest in these questions and abilities?

Two important principles emerge here. First, the best teachers plan backward; they begin with the results they hope to foster. They ask themselves if they want students to recall, comprehend, apply, analyze, synthesize, or evaluate. Sometimes they focus on the kinds of conversations students should be prepared to enter, and with whom (other students, an educated public, policy-makers, researchers, and so on); the types of questions they should learn to answer without resorting to rote memorization; or the human qualities they should develop. "I might begin," one professor told us, "by trying to write down the largest question that the course would address. I would then list the questions that one would need to explore to address the larger issue." The teachers often pressed themselves to higher levels, rejecting their first attempt to raise that "big" question and asking themselves, "what lies behind this question?" Sometimes they pushed themselves to the frontiers of large philosophical questions ("Can humans control their own destiny?").

Second, the question assumes that if teachers expect certain results, the students must believe, or come to believe, that they want to achieve those same ends. We found people who think about how they can help students understand all the beauty and joy of the enterprise before them. They often talked about the excitement they might stir or the curiosity they might provoke. An important part of their planning centered on what they could do in the first meeting with students to win devotion to the goals of the class— that is, what intellectual promises they might make.

2. What reasoning abilities must students have or develop to answer the questions that the course raises?

Because they prize the ability to use evidence in drawing conclusions, the best teachers expect more than some rote memorization of correct answers. Instead, they want to know how to help students reason toward those answers. What does it mean to think like a historian, physicist, chemist, or political scientist? What are the particular abstract reasoning abilities that students must possess to understand certain concepts central to the discipline? Where are the students likely to have the most difficulty in reading or solving problems in the field? How can I encourage them to grapple collectively, to practice their reasoning abilities? How can I provide a sequence of experiences that will encourage students to refine their reasoning abilities?

3. What mental models are students likely to bring with them that I will want them to challenge? How can I help them construct that intellectual challenge?

For Jeanette Norden, it was important to identify the fundamental conceptions that keep students from understanding important ideas, to spell out the new models she hoped they would acquire, and to understand how she could determine if the students had acquired them or at least understood the problems they faced in accepting anything. She carefully planned ways to challenge assumptions and put students in compelling situations in which their existing models would not work.

4. What information will my students need to understand in order to answer the important questions of the course and challenge their assumptions? How will they best obtain that information?

Only here did the teachers consider anything close to the common inquiry, "What will I include in my lectures?" In this case, however, the question begins with what the students need to learn rather than with what the professor intends to do. The focus remains on helping people learn to reason or create, to use new information, not on the need to tell students everything they must know and understand.

This query also challenges much of the traditional perspective on learning. Some professors discuss knowledge as if it is something they "deliver" or "transfer" to students, almost as if they open heads and pour it in. Not surprisingly, they focus on building the explanation that makes the most sense to them rather than on one that will help and encourage students to construct their own explanations, to reason, to draw conclusions, to act. In the model contained in this question, however, students become the actors in the learning process. They obtain information, develop their understanding of it, and learn to use it. "It doesn't matter what I do in class," Ralph Lynn would say, "because the only way you will ever learn is to read and think."

In reality, Lynn and others did think carefully about what they did in class, and this question greatly influenced their choices. Sometimes they decided that they needed to explain something; on other occasions, they taught students how to read more effectively, or asked them to explain key points to each other. Frequently, they helped students reason through ideas and information encountered in reading assignments. Often, then, the question became, "What key information or concepts can I clarify to provide students with foundations (scaffolds) from which they can continue to build their understanding?" (a much richer question than "What will I cover?"). In short, what can we do in class to help students learn outside of class?

5. How will I help students who have difficulty understanding the questions and using evidence and reason to answer them?
Some of the best teachers might plan explanations. Others might devise questions that will help students focus their attention on significant issues, clarify concepts, or emphasize assumptions that they might otherwise ignore. Many professors think about what they can ask students to write that will help and encourage them to grapple with important ideas, applications, implications, and as-

sumptions. What can I show them? What stories can I tell them? What voices do they need to hear besides mine? How can I identify students who will have the most difficulty developing the necessary reasoning skills? How can I create an environment in which students can reason together and challenge each other? While these questions might seem to apply only to weaker students, such was not the case. They applied just as strongly to those who make top grades. "Some students do well in school," one professor told us, "but still do not develop a good understanding or the capacity to think or to think about their own thinking. I'm trying to figure out how to move those students from mere performance to levels of deeper and more meaningful learning." How can I help even the best students to understand more deeply, to refine their reasoning capacities, and to recognize the nature of the learning open to them? Exceptional teachers recognize that sometimes the material creates emotional conflicts that prevent highly capable students from doing well.

6. How will I confront my students with conflicting problems (maybe even conflicting claims about the truth) and encourage them to grapple (perhaps collaboratively) with the issues?

Some professors teach as if their disciplines are essentially a huge body of immutable facts that students must memorize. Such notions are often most fiercely defended in the sciences ("we have certain facts that students must learn; there isn't much room for debate"), but they also exist among historians and other specialists in the social sciences and humanities. This sixth question came from people who had quite different notions about their fields of study—or at least about how it could be learned—ideas that emphasized the constructed and continually revised nature of scholarly knowledge and the importance of helping students construct their own understanding.

Scientists and humanists did, nevertheless, develop dissimilar versions of this epistemology. Humanists, for example, ask this question because they see conflicting claims to the truth that are constantly struggling for recognition and primacy. Scientists raise it because they believe that newer and better information constantly updates theories and data as the discipline struggles to understand nature. They might also invoke this inquiry because they constantly wrestle with the implications and possible applications of the "truths" they have discovered, and they want their students to join that conversation.

Either way, the very best teachers searched for ways to build these conflicts into the structure of the class. Sometimes they would teach the debates, pairing thinkers from opposite positions when reading assignments were made. They might help students understand current scientific conclusions by looking at earlier beliefs that brought us to this intellectual moment. They would help students focus on those points in the history of the discipline when fundamental thinking shifted and then embroil them in the controversies that swirled within those moments. One teacher posed an intriguing and conceptually rich question, worked with the students to help them develop a hypothesis to answer the inquiry, examined with them the evidence that spoke to that hypothesis, and encouraged them to develop additional conjectures that would take that evidence into consideration. Often, the teachers would help students grapple with the implications or applications of scientific truths. Some would ask students to bring, say, two questions to class every day and then use those questions to build a critical conversation.

There were also tactical considerations. How can I best facilitate these discussions and collaborations? What kind of groups will I form or encourage in the class? Will I create them homogeneously or heterogeneously, or will I let the students form them on their own? Will I include some group work in class to help build group cohesion? If I let groups form on their own, what will I do to help shy students find a home?

7. How will I find out what they know already and what they expect from the course, and how will I reconcile any differences between my expectations and theirs?

Anyone who teaches faces a dilemma. On the one hand, we know that people learn most effectively when they are trying to answer their own questions. Yet teachers, not students, generally control the questions, set the educational agenda, design the curriculum and determine its content and goals. And rightfully so, because professors, as experts in their field, have a much better grasp of what learning the discipline might entail. This seventh question tries to reconcile these conflicting demands by searching for and exploring the common ground between instructors and learners.

How will I, early in the term, survey student interest in particular issues or questions? Can I use the Internet to collect that information before the term begins, or pass out index cards during the first session and ask students what they want to know? Will I give my class a list of the major questions that the course will consider and ask them to indicate their interests in these inquiries?

How can I stimulate students to ask good questions and take charge of their own education? Can I get students to talk with each other about their varied interests and, on the basis of those conversations, stimulate broader curiosities that will help me build a community of learners with common interests? How can I help them see the connection between their questions and the issues I have already chosen for the course? Can I, for example, link the questions of the class to some larger issues that already intrigue the students?

Many of the best teachers go even further, asking themselves, Am I prepared to make changes in individual class sessions or in the whole course to connect with my students? How can I pick examples that will be most meaningful to them? Am I willing to tinker with the course as it progresses—to change exams, assignments, or what we do in class—to respond to what I learn about students' interests and knowledge? With a vast amount to learn, can I pick that subset in which students are most interested?

8. *How will I help students learn to learn, to examine and assess their own learning and thinking, and to read more effectively, analytically, and actively?*
Teachers in the study generally assumed that they had some major responsibility to help students become better, self-conscious learners. Part of that effort centered on stimulating thinking about learning and about what it would mean to think using the standards and procedures of the discipline. Can I demonstrate how I learn and solve problems in the discipline? Can I offer any advice, any tricks that will enable students to develop an understanding of important ideas, and to remember what they understand? How did I learn this material? How can I raise questions or pose problems that will stimulate students to think about what it means to learn and how they can improve their learning and thinking?

We found among the most effective teachers a strong desire to help students learn to read in the discipline. That wish emerged, in part, because appropriate reading strategies vary from discipline to discipline. It came also from a recognition that beyond the early grades most students receive little formal help with their reading, even though the sophistication expected increases substantially as they progress through school. Consequently, the best professors looked for suggestions they might make about how to read the scholarship in the field, or questions they might ask to highlight particular analytical strategies. What is unique and distinctive about reading material for this course and how can I break that reading into identifiable strategies? Some of them devised exercises in which groups of students would grapple with a complex text collaboratively. We discovered also a firm intention to structure the course in ways that encouraged students to learn how to learn and to benefit from their own mistakes. That plan led to the next question.

9. How will I find out how students are learning before assessing them, and how will I provide feedback before—and separate from—any assessment of them?

Because many teachers think their primary responsibility is to select good students, they follow a simple pattern: instruct (usually meaning, provide correct answers in the form of oral explanations or lectures) then evaluate. A fundamentally different conception of teaching and students drives this ninth question, and it is the same idea that Richard Light found reflected in the highly effective courses he identified at Harvard. Because the best teachers believe that most students can learn, they look for ways to help all of them do so. They ask how they can encourage students to think aloud and create a nonthreatening atmosphere in which they can do so. They seek ways to give students the opportunity to struggle with their thoughts without facing assessments of their efforts, to try, come up short, receive feedback on their efforts, and try again before facing any "grading."

Traditional grading, as this question recognizes, simply represents an invention, a way of looking at someone else's thoughts and work and categorizing those intellectual products into broad classifications ("A" work, "A-" work, and so on), a device that, in truth, conveys little insights into the qualities and deficiencies of what students are doing. The modern system of grading—the idea of assigning a number or letter to someone's learning—is, of course, a fairly recent invention in higher education. It gained increasing popularity only in the twentieth century as the culture sought ways to certify competence in an increasingly complex and technical world. Within its system, the professor holds a dual role, first, to help students learn, and second, to tell society how much learning has taken place. The intent of this ninth question is to recognize the distinctions between these two responsibilities and to restore the primacy of the first. Thus it seeks ways to provide learners with feedback rather than simply judge their efforts.

What level of interaction can I have with each student? Will I have time to talk with students individually *in addition* to reading their work? What schedule should I follow in meeting with them? What assistance can I give them? If I can't meet with each one, can I meet with them in groups to get at their problems and to understand how they are learning, thinking, and reacting to the class? Can I arrange for students to provide meaningful feedback to each other? What can I do to help improve the quality of that exchange? Can I arrange for other people (for example, graduate students or people who took the class last year) to provide feedback? Can I use class time for students to work on problems in groups and then offer them collective feedback?

10. How will I communicate with students in a way that will keep them thinking?

While this question might lead to an examination of lecture styles and content (a subject explored more fully in Chapter 5), it could also center on any type of communication with students, including brief explanations, moderation of a discussion, or oral instructions. It could also lead some people to examine alternative ways to share ideas and information—on paper, through the Internet, on film or video. Most important, it focuses on stimulating student involvement and attention rather than on the teacher's performance per se; the communication succeeds only if it stimulates students to think.

How can I maintain a conversational tone and still reach all my students? How can I avoid a monotone? How will I provide diversity of sounds, of rhythms, of colors? When will I pause . . . and listen? Is there a provocative question or explanation that will capture their attention? Does my body say the same things that my words do? What visual aids might better engage them? Will I put some items on paper to be distributed in class? When will I distribute those materials to make the greatest impact, to help the students focus? When will I stop talking and let students talk with each other or look at something I've prepared for them? If I write on the board, how can I avoid talking to the wall? How can I be pithy? Where can I avoid clutter in my language? How can I emphasize key points? What do I need to repeat, and how can I say it again without losing the students?

Our subjects usually wanted to promote deep rather than surface or strategic learning, to help students become better thinkers, and to encourage them to grapple with important issues and understand concepts. As they prepared to communicate with students, they kept those goals in mind and let them shape the communication they used.

11. How will I spell out the intellectual and professional standards I will be using in assessing students' work, and why do I use those standards? How will I help students learn to assess their own work using those standards?

"If students can't learn to judge the quality of their own work," Paul Travis argued, "then they haven't really learned." "The standard for good work," another professor told us, "is a way of expressing the very meaning of learning." How can I guide students to look carefully at the thinking and reasoning in which they are engaged? How can I help them understand, appreciate, and adopt the standards of good reasoning that the course expects of them? How can I lead them to compare and contrast their reasoning in this course with thinking they might do in other courses or situations?

12. How will the students and I best understand the nature, progress, and quality of their learning?

Notice that this question doesn't ask how many tests a teacher will give or how the teacher will calculate the final grade. It explores how students develop intellectually, not just how they perform on school work. What are the best indications of how learners understand something? How will we know how they can reason? Educators who use this question expect students to understand their own learning. They might even expect them to help design ways to comprehend it. A trust begins to emerge, as teachers and students listen to each other.

13. How will I create a natural critical learning environment in which I embed the skills and information I wish to teach in assignments (questions and tasks) that students will find fascinating—authentic tasks that will arouse curiosity, challenge students to rethink their assumptions and examine their mental models of reality? How will I create a safe environment in which students can try, fail, receive feedback, and try again?

All the preceding questions center around this key inquiry and its conception of how best to help and encourage people to learn. For the very best teachers, it often led to a highly authentic, fascinating project that would challenge students' thinking. That project became the central feature of the course, but rather than just assigning it, the professors would break it into small yet still meaningful and interesting parts, and constantly attend to helping students keep their focus on the broader goals of their learning.

In fall 1977, Chad Richardson came to the Lower Rio Grande Valley in the southern tip of Texas and began teaching in the sociology program at Pan American University. Polishing off his own graduate studies at the University of Texas at Austin, he was eager to introduce others to the excitement of his discipline. At his new university, most of the students came from the local area; three-quarters spoke Spanish and were of Mexican descent. They had a rich cultural heritage, but by most conventional measures they generally lacked the academic skills necessary to do well in college. A few came from families that had prospered in the local agricultural economy that sprang up along the river. Most students, however, lived closer to the poverty line, and many came from the ranks of the one hundred thousand migrant farm workers in Hidalgo County, people whose labor had created the wealth of the region but who enjoyed few of its benefits. But they were pioneers, often the first in their families to take a college course, and sometimes the first to read and write. The university, with its open admissions policy, cut across a wide swath of SAT scores and high school ranks, but generally didn't attract many students in higher registers.

In this border region, located on the fringes of two national civilizations and not quite comfortable with either, Hispanics valued tradition and culture, yet often found themselves the focus of mean-spirited caricatures that belittled their habits, language, and origins. The twenty percent of the local population that didn't come from Mexican roots—what locals called "Anglos"—sometimes felt isolated and alienated from the local cultures, even though, as a group, they had dominant economic and political power.

Richardson wanted his students to consider one central question and all its major implications: How does society influence individual human behavior, and is that influence greater than the personal and biological forces within each person? Many of them came to the course, he said, convinced that human behavior came only from within. He sought to supplant that paradigm with one that considered the sociological forces that could shape their lives. He also wanted all his students, Mexican Americans and Anglos, to develop an empathetic understanding of the diverse cultural heritage in which they lived, and to emerge from his class with increased abilities—and confidence in those abilities—to think sociologically and to communicate their thoughts to others. That meant they had to learn to think both inductively—to build from specific examples an understanding of important sociological concepts—and deductively—to use those ideas to comprehend new circumstances.

A tall order, but Richardson found solutions in what he thought he knew about natural learning and in his faith in the power of stories. He had thought about the way children learn their native language, and he realized that it came not from memorizing rules but rather from "inductively pulling together patterns from many examples." In sociology, he would help students encounter those many examples as they did original ethnographic research, collecting stories from friends, relatives, and others on both sides of the border: employers of undocumented Mexican workers, smugglers who helped these people enter the United States, immigration officials who apprehended "illegal aliens," Anglos who found themselves in a tiny minority in a Valley high school, Mexican Americans who didn't know Spanish, and others.

On the first day of class he gave students a syllabus with a step-by-step recipe for their projects. It invited rather than commanded, avoiding the language of requirements and setting a tone of positive expectations ("you will be . . ."). In the days to come, Richardson provided them with extensive training on how to conduct interviews, notice patterns, and write a report on their experiences. In class, he discussed important sociological concepts then had the students work in groups to apply those concepts and report back on their efforts. Rather than just "lecturing," however, he engaged classes in discussion, using their experiences to help them understand the fundamental ideas.

Although students responded well to this authentic task, it still smacked of so much schoolwork. In 1983, Richardson began to change that, providing them with an authentic outlet for their efforts. He started an archive of the students' ethnographic research and arranged with a local newspaper to publish some of the stories they were collecting. He also shared that work with incoming classes, allowing them to see what earlier students had accomplished.

Initially the assignment sometimes intimidated them, but once they saw what other students had done they became more willing to try. As they engaged in the project, they became empowered by the way it gave meaning to their own culture and region. Students' writing improved dramatically, as did their reading comprehension, their understanding of sociological concepts, and their powers of observation, analysis, and synthesis. "Retention tends to be more secure," Richardson concluded, "when we are led with examples to form a conclusion than when we are simply presented with a concept and an example or two to illustrate it." Self-esteem improved as students reported greater confidence in their own abilities to understand sophisticated concepts, to apply those ideas, to collect and analyze data, and to communicate their thinking. A growing number went to graduate school in sociology and other fields, and one of them became the chair of the sociology department at Texas A&M University. In 1999, Richardson and 350 of his students published a collection of their work with the University of Texas Press.[2]

For Richardson, the greatest achievement came with the broad band of students who experienced "greater awareness of the rich cultural heritage of the region." The experience, he concluded, "enhanced acceptance of diversity, a sense of historical 'place,' and promoted self-esteem."

Richardson came to the Valley hoping to continue his own research while teaching eight to ten classes a year. Rather than seeing a conflict between these two enterprises, he discovered that both research and teaching are concerned with learning, and he explored ways in which the learning of professors and students could benefit each other.

At the Rhode Island School of Design, landscape architecture, architecture, and industrial design students traditionally complete individual projects that they submit to the faculty for a grade. "Much of the work (in school and in the profession) is done in a linear fashion," Charlie Cannon noted. "Architects do their part, pass it along to landscape architects and industrial engineers, but with little integration of all three perspectives throughout the process." He and his colleagues wanted to help students learn to collaborate, to integrate disciplines, to move beyond their immediate areas of expertise, and even to help define new ways for the profession to think about how large-scale public projects get done—whose voices are heard and how a cacophony of words and ideas gets turned into something concrete. He wanted students to learn to consider environmental, social, economic, community, and political issues in their designs.

In the innovative studio that emerged—a course for both undergraduates and graduate industrial designers and building and landscape architects—Cannon made several key decisions that fundamentally changed the educational experience. First, he changed his role from judge of some final product to facilitator and one-on-one coach. Second, he arranged for students to work collaboratively on a large and complex project, constantly sharing ideas and information from all their fields of study. Everything they learned was embedded in the pursuit of an intriguing collective goal, something authentic with hands-on experience. Third, he helped them do research on a variety of social, economic, environmental, community, and political issues. Most important, he ultimately gave students control over the class and the work—even though he had selected their project.

To give them that control, Cannon carefully chose a project that "appealed to students." On the first day of class, he tried to help all students understand the heavy demands of time they faced and the collaborative nature of the project. He also stressed that their work was authentic and would make a difference. Ideas they generated could be implemented in a real project; and, most important, with their pioneering explorations of collaboration and the consideration of multiple perspectives, they would reshape the profession. Finally, he left them to decide whether to participate in this demanding, "often grueling," but rewarding experience. As the semester unfolded, Cannon continued to shift power to the students until "they had assumed ownership." At first he spelled out what they must achieve, but then he left them in charge of means. He invited students to pick an individual topic they would explore thoroughly ("everything from land art to technical solutions"). For the remainder of the semester, every student became the class expert on a single topic. "If we needed to know about the migration patterns of rattlesnakes, we knew who could tell us," Cannon explained. Once students finished their research, they reported back to the class, grilled each other, and synthesized their findings into several large boards that remained on display.

Because collaborative work was new to them, Cannon continually emphasized the shifting roles they must play: facilitator, transcriber, someone to make sure everyone is included in the discussion, and a person or two who "attends to the emotional tenor of the group." He emphasized the need to respect one another's work, and reminded them that they were "all in the same boat," researching topics about which they knew little.

After four weeks in the library and classroom, students visited the physical site of the project—a proposed waste-treatment facility in New York harbor, for example—then toured other related places: a town dump, recycling center, and the office of engineers who make products out of recycled materials. "Their book-based learning," Cannon noted, "was suddenly connected to how dirty things might be on the ground." They drove around local neighborhoods, looked through phone books at the distributions of businesses in the area, and studied aerial and zoning maps. At the end of their tours, Cannon invited six to twelve other people—community activists, an environmental crusader, planners, architects, artists, and even students from other schools—to join them in two days of brainstorming about possible solutions. He wanted his students to "spell out the broadest array" of possible approaches, to "immerse themselves in the soup of nonconclusion," and only during the last day to contemplate implications and combine their thoughts into "constellations" of ideas. "They were encouraged to develop ideas that are as physically different from each other as possible," Cannon explained, "so that they could begin to recognize that no one solution is the sole answer to the problem."

Then came the Master Planning Stage. "At this point," Cannon explained, "I lock them in a room and say, 'it's not likely that any of our ideas thus far are the right answer. We need to develop design guidelines or philosophies for attacking this work and I want you to come up with those ideas, to decide what direction the studio will go.' I ask them to work out what the studio project will be, and then I leave the room." At that crucial moment, the students design the problem they will collectively tackle over the remaining weeks of the term. "Now the year belongs to them. They have usurped my limited problem, reframed it, and defined the goals of the studio." Ultimately, they consult again with outside experts, pick individual parts of the "master narrative" they each will pursue, and share their work with one another.

The students do not meet many of the traditional standards of a design studio. They do not have time to produce the kind of polished work more conventional studios might churn out. Yet they learn how to work collaboratively, to research and consider a host of related issues, including environmental ones, to weigh multiple perspectives, and to define the nature of the problems. Cannon redefined what he wanted students to learn from the class and then created an experience that fostered the achievement of those goals, throwing aside conventions about what should be done in the course and what students should accomplish.

Highly effective teachers design better learning experiences for their students in part because they conceive of teaching as fostering learning. Everything they do stems from their strong concern for and understanding of the development of their students. They follow few traditions blindly and recognize when change in the conventional course is both necessary and possible. The baker's dozen can help us remember what to ask when we plan a course, but if we expect to learn from the practices and thinking of highly effective teachers, we must do more than become routine experts, applying and perfecting some inherited pattern—even if it comes from the best. We must use their approaches to help build our own understanding of powerful learning environments and the adaptive spirit and expertise to toss aside inhibiting conventions in search of better solutions.

WHAT DO THEY EXPECT
OF THEIR STUDENTS?

Claude Steele confronted a problem many of us face in our classrooms. The social psychologist from Stanford knew the bitter stereotypes that said African American and Hispanic students generally cannot do well in college and that women cannot do mathematics and physics. He knew also the national statistics that fed those prejudices: across the country African Americans and Hispanics fail gateway courses more frequently than do other students, while few women become mathematicians or physicists. Steele refused, however, to accept either the sexist or the racist explanation for this disturbing pattern.

He knew that the long night of racism, sexism, segregation, and discrimination had left its mark. People who face repeated messages that they are inferior in a certain kind of activity (schoolwork, for example) will often decide to drop out and build a life in another area. Furthermore, black and Hispanic children are more likely than their European American peers to face inferior schools and have inadequate preparation for college. Yet neither of those factors explains why *as a group* (with numerous individual exceptions) even well-prepared, ambitious, self-confident middle-and upper-class African American students lag behind similar groups of European American students.

Could it be, the Stanford psychologist began to wonder, that negative social stereotypes still had an influence on their targets even when ethnic minorities and women consciously rejected them?[1] Steele suspected that they did. Moreover, he surmised—because his evidence pointed to this startling conclusion—that the negative stereotypes sometimes had the strongest influence on students who had all the confidence in the world, had not internalized any sense of inferiority, often had excellent preparations, and really cared about doing well academically.

He theorized that when victims of negative stereotypes face a task that popular prejudice says they are not very good at but that they nonetheless want to do and believe they can do, they cannot escape the shadow of the beliefs around them. If the task is particularly difficult and stressful, that pressure will trigger at least a subconscious reminder of the stereotype. "If I don't solve this problem," they might think, "other people will believe the common image is true." The more they care about doing well in that domain, the more such a thought bothers them. At minimum, it distracts them; at worst, it prods them to prove the popular prejudice wrong. Either way, their awareness of the negative stereotype adds a level of anxiety that others do not face, and the resulting stress slows and harms performance, which in turn produces even more anguish, causing additional reminders, and so forth.

Steele knew, for example, that numerous studies had found that women do just as well in mathematics as do men *up to a certain level of difficulty.* Beyond that threshold, most females perform poorly. For decades, many educated men had concluded that something in the gender explained the differences. Steele reasoned, however, that both men and women begin to feel a little anxiety when faced with difficult math problems they want to solve, but for men that anxiety comes from the math problems themselves. Women, by contrast, begin to face an extra burden as the initial stress triggers a reminder of the negative stereotype: "What are others thinking of me, and what must I do to prove them wrong?" Steele called this feeling "stereotype vulnerability" and explained that it often results when individuals feel they "could be judged or treated in terms of a negative stereotype or could do something that would confirm that stereotype" in the minds of those around them.

As most women try to disprove the common prejudice about

their ability, they become even more anxious, especially if they put great stock in doing well in math and believe on some level that they can. Steele said it just recently: "A person has to care about a domain in order to be disturbed by the prospect of being stereotyped in it." Thus a woman who does well in mathematics in high school and the early college years or a black student who excels in any subject may dream of a future in the field, but it is those dreams that stimulate what Steele called "vigilant worry that their future will be compromised by society's perception and treatment of their group." The more they care, the more vulnerable they become to stereotype threat, and it is success not failure that makes them care.

Steele and other researchers discovered that if they can keep people from thinking that someone else might be viewing them through the lens of a negative stereotype, they can significantly change what those people accomplished. Steele found, for example, that if he could convince women who took difficult mathematics examinations that everyone connected with the test assumed they would perform as well as men, that they did.[2] In another experiment, he and Joshua Aronson brought black students at Stanford to their laboratory and gave them questions from the verbal portion of the Graduate Record Examination. They told one group that the questions tested their verbal ability; a second group, that it was a "laboratory task that was used to study how certain problems are generally solved" and, by implication, had nothing to do with their intelligence. That simple change in explanation produced dramatically different results. The students who thought that their verbal ability was in question performed far less well even though the two groups had indistinguishable backgrounds.[3]

The Stanford researchers even found that they could create a stereotype threat among people who have traditionally faced only positive social images about themselves in some domain. White males, for example, face no popular notion that "their kind" can't do math. Yet the researchers could make European American male students with good grades in advanced math courses perform less well on a difficult test if they simply told them that Asian students generally did better on the exam than did "white students." Suddenly, they too faced the possibility that if they stumbled on the exam, others would see them as inferior to some other group.[4]

What does this research mean and how does it relate to the study on highly effective teachers? It seems to be connected to a debate that often emerges between the kind of teachers we studied and some of their colleagues. Here's how: If you believe the faculty scuttlebutt that pervades many college campuses, the best way to achieve a reputation for good teaching—or at least get high marks from student raters—is to offer a fluff course requiring students to do little work. Some professors are convinced that the path to teaching awards is paved with lower standards and expectations, and that their own refusal to compromise accounts for the miserable showings they muster on student ratings. Yet the work that social psychologists have done with stereotype vulnerability and our research on highly effective teachers seriously challenge such simple notions.

By any reasonable measure, the best teachers expect "more" from their students, but we also found many less successful teachers who try to challenge their students by piling on the work. For these people, asking students to do more often does produce lower ratings *and perhaps less learning* because the learners emerge exhausted and alienated. It is easy to conclude from such examples that the scuttlebutt is true, but that reasoning misses some important points and often misleads beginning and experienced teachers alike. Why do some teachers expect more and get students to produce it with great satisfaction while others fail miserably with what they regard as "higher" standards? Is there something distinctive in the nature of the "more" that our subjects expect? Do the highly successful teachers handle the assignments differently, or possess some other quality that accounts for the results they achieve?

We found an intricate web of beliefs, conceptions, attitudes, and practices driving the accomplishments of the best teachers and their students. Each strand of the web depends on all the others for its potency. Separated from each other they can even seem trivial and superficial. To understand what makes some teaching exceptional, we must know the individual strands and how they nourish one another. We begin with a series of attitudes and tendencies that underlie teachers' efforts.

First, the best teachers tended to look for and appreciate the individual value of each student. Rather than separating them into winners and losers, geniuses and dullards, good students and bad, they looked for the abilities that any person brought to the table. Paul Baker, the highly successful drama professor from Texas, said it repeatedly. "Every student is unique and brings contributions that no one else can make."

Second, and this is the first direct connection to the research on stereotypes, they had great faith in students' ability to achieve. Steele's work should help us understand the extra burdens faced by anyone who has been a target of some pervasive negative stereotype, and the especially onerous burdens female students encounter in certain subjects and African Americans and some other minorities carry in all academic pursuits—burdens that most white males in our society do not experience. No other use of Steele's findings should distract from the significance of that central message. But his research and the inquiries of others also reinforce a key point emerging from our conversations with highly effective teachers: Students will be buoyed by positive expectations that are genuine, challenging yet realistic, and that take their work seriously.

A few years ago Geoffrey Cohen, one of Steele's colleagues, conducted an experiment that reflected much of what I'm saying here. He asked bright students at Stanford, both blacks and whites, to submit essays about their favorite teacher for possible inclusion in a journal. He wanted to know what kind of feedback might be most stimulating, so he asked each student to return in a few days for some response to their efforts. To tell students (even subconsciously) that reviewers would know their "race," he took a Polaroid picture of each person and stapled it to the front page of the essay.

When they returned to get feedback, Cohen tried three different approaches. In one version, he simply told students what was wrong with their essays. In another, he offered a few compliments before making any criticisms. He noticed that regardless of what he did some students went home and fixed their essays; others never returned, but the method of feedback didn't affect how many or which students came back. He also noticed that neither approach stimulated many black students to respond while the white students usually returned with both approaches.

Cohen reasoned that stereotype threat had led most of the black subjects to think that his assessments stemmed from the prejudice that African Americans can't write well. Meanwhile, the European Americans took the advice at face value. To test his theory, he had to find some way to bridge the gap and get black students to trust his recommendations. He began telling them that the journal had high standards but with some revisions they could meet them. As Steele put it, that approach, "the combination of high standards and assurance, was like water on parched land, a much needed but seldom received balm" for the minority students. It clearly said that they would be judged not by some negative stereotype but by high standards and that their mentor actually had faith that they could meet those requirements. With this third kind of mentoring, black students took their essays home, applied the advice, and returned with much better work than before.[5]

The best teachers tended to use the third method with all their students. They set high standards and conveyed a strong trust in their students' abilities to meet them. Yet that trust didn't stand alone; it emerged in the context of something else that the stereotype research supported. Because these teachers understood that fear and anxiety can reduce the capacity to think, they promoted intellectual excitement and curiosity rather than worry and doubt over "making the grade." That effort appeared in everything they did, including the way they assessed their students, a subject I explore more fully in the last chapter. While others might emphasize the amount of work they could pile on, the people in the study stressed the ability to create exceptional works of art or scholarship, to reason well and carefully, to comprehend complex issues and problems, to collect and use evidence, to solve problems, and to do whatever the most accomplished scholars, practitioners, and artists in the field might do outside the course. The "more" in the hands of these people flowed from the highest intellectual, artistic, and moral standards rather than from demands that had meaning only in the context of being in school. "I want to know," one student told us, "that the assignment benefits me personally and intellectually and that it's not just done for the sake of school or a grade."

Trust in the students also depended on the teacher's rejection of power over them. The educators we studied invited people to pursue ambitious goals and promised to help them achieve, but they left learners in control of their own education, avoiding any sense of "commanding the troops into a tough battle." Thus the "more" was as much a promise they made ("here's what you will be able to learn/achieve in this class") as it was a set of expectations. While the teachers seemed at times almost incapable of imagining that their students could not think and act on the highest level, they also could not imagine forcing anyone to do so. "What you bring to this class is yourself and your desire to participate," Paul Baker would tell his students, "and what you do in here depends finally upon that."[6]

Trust, rejection of power, and setting standards that represented authentic goals rather than schoolwork are apparent in the kind of syllabus the best teachers tended to use. This "promising syllabus," as we dubbed it, had three major parts. First, the instructor would lay out the promises or opportunities that the course offered to students. What kind of questions would it help students answer? What kind of intellectual, physical, emotional, or social abilities would it help them develop? That section represented an invitation to a feast, giving students a strong sense of control over whether they accepted. Second, the teacher would explain what the students would be doing to realize those promises (formerly known as requirements), avoiding the language of demands, and again giving the students a sense of control over their own education. They could decide to pursue the goals on their own, without taking the course, but if they decided to stay in the class, they needed to do certain things to achieve. Third, the syllabus summarized how the instructor and the students would understand the nature and progress of the learning. This was far more than an exposition of grading policies; it was the beginning of a dialogue in which both students and instructors explored how they would understand learning, so they could both make adjustments as they went and evaluate the nature of the learning by the end of the term. Because students encountered the syllabus at the beginning of the term, it became a powerful influence on setting high standards and encouraging people to achieve them.

Finally, trust succeeded because it was realistic. It demanded an ambitious yet honest appraisal of what any one person could do, and that required a sophisticated understanding of both individuals and the social forces that could influence how students performed. We found professors who took great pains to explore their students' learning, to analyze their work carefully, to think extensively about what and how different people could learn, and even to design particular assignments to fit the needs, interests, and current abilities of each student. Even in large classes where it became impossible to know every single student, they explored composite pictures that could help them think about the types of students populating their classes.

The success of the teachers' analysis—and this is the key point here—rested on a fairly advanced understanding of the external forces that could determine academic success. Few of the outstanding teachers knew about Claude Steele's work when we started the study (although more have learned about it since then), but all of them seemed to grasp that far more than some "native intellect" influenced who did what in school and that sometimes conventional measures of the best and brightest fail to find exceptionally talented students. For example, when we shared the Cohen story with people outside the study, many of them argued, as one person put it, "if you have students like the white students at Stanford, it doesn't matter how you teach them." To these people, the secret to good teaching was simply to find brilliant learners.

In contrast, exceptional teachers emphasized an analysis that went something like this: Much has conditioned the majority students at Stanford to excel academically, including their position in society and years of habituation in highly competitive and demanding schools. Furthermore, they would argue, those students have generally known few stereotype threats that might change helpful advice into something they could not trust. Many of them have lived all their academic lives in the lap of high expectations and confidence in their abilities. "If it didn't make any difference in the Cohen experiment what kind of feedback they received," one professor argued, "that was simply because they had overstocked reservoirs of assurance from which to drink. External factors from the past helped shape their success, and external factors that the instructor can create can make a big difference now, either to stimulate students who have never had much help or to mess up students who already have many advantages."

The perception that external factors do make a difference and the rich understanding of how some of those forces work helped give our subjects the ability to expect more and get it. In general, they looked for the diamonds in the rough, took all their students seriously, and treated each one with respect. When they offered suggestions, they could convince their students through the sheer weight of their own sincerity—an earnestness born from the perceptions described here and from their diligence in getting to know their students—that their critique didn't intend to judge anyone's soul or worth as a human being. It was, instead, based on the high standards of the best scientific, scholarly, or artistic thinking, and came not because the professor thought less of the student but because he or she believed the student had the capacity to benefit from the advice. While some of their colleagues wanted to work only with a conventional version of the best and brightest and even sometimes talked contemptuously about students whose backgrounds were different (like the dean we encountered who spoke disparagingly of the academic worth and intellectual ability of Chinese graduate students who spoke English with strong "foreign" accents, or the New England-educated English professor who told us her students couldn't learn because they had "hillbilly accents"), the very best teachers had a deeper vision of ultimate quality that left them with a strong faith in their students' abilities. It was that faith and vision that guided their practices.

This is not to suggest that the teachers we studied thought all students could do all things. Certainly they showed a willingness to tell students when they might be better suited to a field other than medicine or acting or whatever. Yet they offered that advice with care and humility while recognizing that social prejudices can easily cloud and shape the most rational conclusions. "Our ideas about who belongs in school," one professor told us, "are too often rooted in prejudices about class and place and even language—let alone about race or ethnicity. When I make judgments about students' suitability for the next level of study in my field—as I do every time I assign a grade or counsel a student about her career—I have to make sure I have derived whatever puny stab I can make at a good decision from good data and good reasoning. Thus, I must worry about the kind of examinations I give, how I interpret the results of those tests, and what else I might use to 'grade' a student."

When students had difficulty in class, the best professors looked for problems in their courses first rather than in their students' preparation or intelligence. They asked themselves how they expected students to react to their courses, what they could do to build on fascinations that might already exist, and how they could overcome difficulties with both motivation and comprehension. They carefully identified solvable problems with students' learning and constructed systematic ways for students to overcome those problems. "I have thought a lot about where my students might encounter the biggest difficulties in understanding," Suhail Hanna, a highly successful English professor in Pennsylvania, told us. "I want to know what is going to seem strange to them and what is familiar so I can make special efforts to connect the two together."

What does all this mean in terms of specific practices? Does it mean that the best teachers avoided timed tests because they were too arbitrary, too tied to the course rather than a reflection of the way most of life works? For some, it certainly did; for others, no. Some teachers gave take-home examinations while others gave students "as long as they needed to finish the final." Most never used the common practice of "counting off" for late papers, but some of them certainly did (more on this in the last chapter). "I give my students control over their own lives," one person reported. "If they take more time, they must realize that they are taking time away from the rest of their lives. They must develop a sense of responsibility to themselves."

The magic does not, however, lie in any one of these practices. I cannot stress enough the simple yet powerful notion that the key to understanding the best teaching can be found not in particular practices or rules but in the *attitudes* of the teachers, in their *faith* in their students' abilities to achieve, in their *willingness* to take their students seriously and to let them assume control of their own education, and in their *commitment* to let all policies and practices flow from central learning objectives and from a mutual respect and agreement between students and teachers.

"She told us the first day," one student related to us in a theme we heard repeatedly, "that the choice was ours. No one had a gun at our head forcing us to get an education . . . We knew she wanted to help us, not control us, and that gave me a lot of confidence that I could do really well."

"I had a teacher once," another student offered in contrast, "who thought she was god's gift to the academic world . . . she thought she was so demanding but she would just insult students right and left. One student asked her how he might write a better paper and she said, 'don't presume you can write a better paper than this. You're not that smart.' That's just not right," she concluded. "The best teachers I had always made you feel good about yourself and your abilities."

Paul Baker often told his students, "The main focus of the course is on developing creative people, giving them confidence in themselves. We are not trying to force you into some kind of mold; on the contrary, we are trying to help you escape."[7]

Susan Wiltshire, a classics professor at Vanderbilt, captured a sentiment we heard often. Her classes, she explained, were in her view like a great meal she had prepared, and she simply wished to invite her students to the dinner table. While others might confront students with the grit of a drill sergeant or as if they were challenging them to a duel, the best teachers offered biscuits and grits for every class.

EXPECTING MORE FROM STUDENTS WITH LOW GRADES

Students in the biological sciences at Northwestern University must take a year-long, sophomore-level course that lays the foundation for all their subsequent work in the field. It is the gateway to graduate and medical school, and over the years, it has acquired a reputation as a demanding and, at times, exhausting experience. The faculty will often note with pride that the average grade is usually at least half a letter lower than the collective GPAs of the students in the class. More than three hundred people regularly sign up for the course and pack themselves into a large lecture hall three times a week to hear a parade of scientists discuss various topics. They also attend weekly laboratory sessions.

When Larry Pinto began teaching in the course in the early 1990s, he and his colleagues were concerned about a broad pattern they observed. Very few, if any, African American, Hispanic, or Native American students ever made higher than a C in the course and most of them failed. When they looked at these students' overall academic records, they found SAT scores, high school grades, and other credentials that suggested these students should have done quite well. Northwestern has tough admissions requirements and they had all met those standards, but they were still failing Biology B10 in alarming numbers. Furthermore, Pinto learned, similar gaps existed between African Americans and other students at most other highly selective universities.

Pinto knew the implications of such numbers. "I want my research labs to look like a cross-section of society," he said, "but they won't if whole segments of the population face insurmountable obstacles." Because the course was a gateway to medical school, the gap meant that few minority students would become physicians. He and his colleagues rejected a racist explanation for the findings and began looking for other answers. Eventually, they turned to Steele's work and the ideas and programs that the mathematician Uri Treisman had fashioned at Berkeley and the University of Texas at Austin. Treisman had confronted similar patterns among African American students in calculus, and he had erased much of the gap with a program that invited minority students into honors workshops rather than into remedial classes. Steele's theories and research certainly supported such a counter-intuitive step. If these students were performing poorly because they suffered from stereotype vulnerability—which they apparently did—a remedial program would only make matters worse, reinforcing the notion that society thought they couldn't make the grade in regular classes. An invitation to an honors workshop, however, would do the opposite, expressing faith that the students could succeed with the highest standards. The biologists were impressed with what they learned and soon carved out their own "Treisman-type" program, but with some important twists.

In fall 1997 they invited all students in Biology B10—including minority students—to participate in advanced conceptual workshops. Pinto made a special effort to reach populations of students like the minority students who had a history of doing poorly in the class, in essence saying to them that he had great faith in their ability to do advanced work. If they joined the program, they would meet once a week in groups of five to seven to tackle conceptually rich advanced problems in biology. Treisman had used graduate students to facilitate those sessions, but the Northwestern biologists, working with a small graduate program, decided to use carefully selected undergraduates who had taken the course the year before. They wanted students who had done well and who had "strong people skills." They eventually asked the teaching center to train these students in advanced facilitation techniques ("ask questions rather than explain"), then they met with the facilitators once a week to go over the problems.

For the next two years, the biologists ran a controlled experiment. They accepted only half the volunteers into the program. Wendi Born, a graduate student in psychology who took on the project for her Ph.D. thesis, created matched pairs between the accepted and the excluded and followed the progress of the two groups. They also made sure that each workshop group looked like the broader society, with usually one or two minority students in each section.[8]

Students in the program did all the work the other students were expected to do and met for two additional hours each week in their volunteer workshops. In those sessions, they wrestled with the problem of the week, struggling with concepts and their implications and applications. Pinto occasionally met with the facilitators, sometimes over dinner in his home, and followed the progress of the program. Students taught students. They struggled to address authentic and intriguing problems in a community of like-minded colleagues. The facilitators occasionally brought food to the sessions and tried to create a sense of camaraderie. The program demanded a higher level of thinking than did the traditional course, but it also gave students control over their own education. They were recruited into the program vigorously but with a strong message of trust in their abilities and judgments.

The results were staggeringly successful for all ethnic groups in the program. Across the board, scores on examinations rose substantially for the participants, and the differences in ethnic groups largely disappeared. They outperformed their matches outside the program. Furthermore, both the facilitators and the workshop participants reported considerably higher interests in the biological sciences than did other students in the class. The workshop students also reported spending less total time on biology than did students outside the experiment, suggesting that "time on task" alone could not explain the improvements. Perhaps most impressive, the improvements generally continued to grow as the year progressed. The following year Pinto and his colleagues repeated the experiment, this time with a slightly larger group, and found much the same results. After two years of controlled experiments, they opened the program to every student in the class. Although they no longer had a control group, they could compare participants with those who didn't volunteer and with the historic performances of other students with similar backgrounds. They continued to observe the same phenomenally positive results.

FUNDAMENTAL IDEAS ABOUT LEARNING

The exceptional qualities and practices discussed thus far—the view that every student brings something special to the table, faith in abilities, concentration on outcomes, rejection of power in favor of creating opportunities, and the perception that external factors do make a difference—rest on an even more fundamental bedrock of ideas about the nature and meaning of learning. Simply put, the best teachers believe that learning involves both personal and intellectual development and that neither the ability to think nor the qualities of being a mature human are immutable. People can change, and those changes—not just the accumulation of information—represent true learning. More than anything else this central set of beliefs distinguishes the most effective teachers from many of their colleagues.

To understand these ideas more fully and how they contrast with conventional notions, let's return to a discussion introduced in Chapter 2. Recall that we found many less successful instructors who think of memory as a storage unit and intelligence as the capacity to use the information in that tank. In their minds, some people simply have both big tanks and great power to retrieve and use the contents of those containers, and other people don't. Because they believe that there is little if anything that anyone can do to expand either memory or intelligence, they see limited responsibilities for themselves and their colleagues. For some, that implies that they should, as several people put it, "get out of the way of bright students and they will learn on their own." For most, it means that they need only provide bright students with the information necessary to make good decisions.

Contrast these views of intelligence with those of the most successful instructors, and consider the implications such notions have for pedagogical practice. If you believe, as our subjects tended to do, that people construct models of reality rather than simply store or "absorb" knowledge, you are more likely to ask how that construction takes place and how it might be improved. You can then ask how people use those models and their constituent parts to make decisions and to reason, and how they might develop better ways to do so. You no longer concentrate on the ability to remember information, but recognize that the power to remember increases as comprehension and the use of that understanding in reasoning grows. From such perspectives, you can begin to ask how mental models and their use shape how people think, act, and feel, and whether and how models of reality, reasoning capacities, emotions, and actions influence one another. You might even ask how people can use, control, and even change their emotions, attitudes, and values, and how the habits of the heart might shape the capacity to understand and to apply any comprehension with compassion and decency.

What begins to emerge is a model of education in which learners do more than accumulate information; they undergo deep-seated changes, transformations that affect both the habits of the heart and mind and the capacity for continued growth. "Everything you learn," Ralph Lynn often said, "influences who you are and what you can do."

Thus the best teachers develop rich notions about what it means to get an education, ideas that are deeply integrated with their beliefs about the capacity of humans to learn, grow, and change. Those notions and convictions promise great achievements for students, and those promises powerfully influence students' actions. They also provide professors with a deep understanding of both the nature of learning and the conditions in which it is likely to flourish. That comprehension enables them to fashion the best learning environments, to shape and remold, to make good decisions about every aspect of teaching, and to respond to problems creatively and effectively. Success breeds success. Because the methods work in helping students achieve, students develop faith in their instructors, and that trust becomes its own force. In the end, no one of these factors stands alone. They all feed on one another.

These patterns are most visible in efforts to promote both intellectual and personal development.

Intellectual Development

Many outstanding teachers think of their courses as ways to help students learn to reason well and to join a conversation that flourishes among people who do. Two questions stand at the heart of this enterprise: What reasoning abilities will students need to possess or develop to answer the questions the discipline raises? How can I cultivate the habits of mind that will lead to constant use of those intellectual skills?

Answers to the first question defy easy summary. Not all disciplines stress the same reasoning abilities, but some broad patterns emerged among those we interviewed, inventories of reasoning that Arnold Arons, a physicist at the University of Washington, captured quite well. Arons argued that critical thinking entails, at minimum, a series of ten reasoning abilities and habits of thought:

1. Consciously raising the questions "What do we know . . . ? How do we know . . . ? Why do we accept or believe . . . ? What is the evidence for . . . ?" when studying some body of material or approaching a problem.
2. Being clearly and explicitly aware of gaps in available information. Recognizing when a conclusion is reached or a decision made in absence of complete information and being able to tolerate the ambiguity and uncertainty. Recognizing when one is taking something on faith without

having examined the "How do we know . . . ? Why do we believe . . . ?" questions.

3. Discriminating between observation and inference, between established fact and subsequent conjecture.

4. Recognizing that words are symbols for ideas and not the ideas themselves. Recognizing the necessity of using only words of prior definition, rooted in shared experience, in forming a new definition and in avoiding being misled by technical jargon.

5. Probing for assumptions (particularly the implicit, unarticulated assumptions) behind a line of reasoning.

6. Drawing inferences from data, observations, or other evidence and recognizing when firm inferences cannot be drawn. This subsumes a number of processes such as elementary syllogistic reasoning (e.g., dealing with basic propositional "if . . . then" statements), correlational reasoning, recognizing when relevant variables have or have not been controlled.

7. Performing hypothetico-deductive reasoning; that is, given a particular situation, applying relevant knowledge of principles and constraints and visualizing, in the abstract, the plausible outcomes that might result from various changes one can imagine to be imposed on the system.

8. Discriminating between inductive and deductive reasoning; that is, being aware when an argument is being made from the particular to the general or from the general to the particular.

9. Testing one's own line of reasoning and conclusions for internal consistency and thus developing intellectual self-reliance.

10. Developing self-consciousness concerning one's own thinking and reasoning processes.[9]

When we share this list with faculty members across a variety of disciplines, it always strikes a responsive chord. If they do not know Arons, many people swear that he must be from their discipline. Both people within and outside the study have had similar reactions, but there is a difference. Most distinctively, our subjects more frequently identified the same critical thinking abilities as major learning objectives of their courses. If they didn't embrace this litany of reasoning abilities, they had one of their own. Furthermore, they did not see a legitimate separation between learning the "facts" and learning to reason with those facts. Rather than trying to teach the facts to students devoid of any reasoning (as if instructors could simply pour those facts into the students), they integrated explanations with questions and problems.

Thus answers to the second question began with one word: *practice*. Give students many opportunities to use their reasoning abilities as they tackle fascinating problems and receive challenges to their thinking. Ask them to consider the implications of their reasoning, implications for themselves, for the way they view the world, for policy debates, for significant philosophical questions, or even for moral or religious issues. Treat the course as a window through which students can begin to see what questions the discipline raises; what information, inquiries, and reasoning skills it employs to answer those questions; what intellectual standards it uses to test proposed answers and to weigh conflicting claims about the "truth." Help students learn to assess their own work using those standards, to become aware of how they think within the discipline, and to compare that thinking with the way they reach conclusions in other disciplines. Ask them about their assumptions and about the concepts and evidence they employ in their reasoning.

Ken Seeskin, a professor of philosophy, asks students to wrestle with major philosophical issues. He seeks to "convince students that the issues are still worth fighting over, that the theories are not ancient relics but positions people may still want to advocate." He pits authors against each other, pairing each thinker with another who takes a different view. He thereby "forces students not only to learn about but to choose between" Plato and Aristotle, Anselm or Aquinas, Kant or Mill. "If great thinkers felt the excitement of entering controversies and refuting opponents," Seeskin concludes, "why should students not be given a taste of the same thing?" In his view, "advocacy generates controversy, and controversy arouses interest."[10]

Seeskin and other exceptional teachers do ask students to take and defend a position in class discussions or in papers and other projects, but they don't just ask them to reason well and then judge their efforts. They provide them with support and constructive criticism, delaying any grading until the students have had plenty of chances to practice and get feedback. That means they must allow their students to express their views while they are still learning. "Some professors argue that they don't want to hear their students talk about a subject because they don't know enough," one teacher explained. "But I always think of piano teachers; they would never keep their students away from the keyboard simply because those pupils couldn't yet play Mozart. Sure they have to endure a lot of bad notes, but they would never push someone off the bench and refuse to let them play until they somehow became better."

Highly effective teachers must choose questions and issues carefully and select common readings even more cautiously. They pay attention to the kind of analysis students will have to do in a given assignment, and they sequence materials to give students an opportunity to build their skills: easier reading first, more difficult later. They often choose highly provocative articles for early readings, and rather than simply listing requirements, they pose questions the way any good discussion leader might, offering the assignments as resources to pursue those inquiries. They don't discuss readings with students; they get them involved in thinking about issues, taking positions, and drawing from their readings to make arguments and solve problems. The most effective teachers avoid like the plague the perennially favorite question, "Who can tell me what this article said?"

Finally, the best educators often teach students how to read the materials. Ralph Lynn developed extensive routines to show students how to examine and analyze a book before they read it. Others teach students how to recognize arguments, distinguish between evidence and conclusions, comprehend the kind of evidence offered (for example, inferred or observed), recognize that agreements and disagreements can emerge in both belief and attitude, understand what kinds of questions need to be asked for each type of evidence and disagreement, identify assumptions, and explore the implications of conclusions. "Students didn't learn how to read scholarly papers in grade school," one teacher told us, "but they usually get little training beyond that level on how to read."

Personal Development

Jeanette Norden has long been interested in helping her medical students acquire exceptional clinical reasoning skills. To that end, she helps them understand an enormous body of material and develop the capacity to use that information in making diagnoses. On examinations, she presents students with real cases and asks them clinically relevant questions about the cases, questions that reflect the thinking processes they will need as physicians. For example, instead of just asking about facts, she might also ask, "What are the two most likely hypotheses? And why do you think so?" Each test is comprehensive and the final can count for a sizeable portion of their grade, giving students opportunities to learn from their mistakes.

In the early 1990s she began to realize, however, that such an education, while necessary, was insufficient. She discovered that many of her future physicians had enormous difficulty confronting death and the strong emotions of patients and families. They often failed to realize that surviving family members needed attention too, or they did not understand appropriate ways to express their compassion. She found a disturbing number of residents and physicians retreating into cold detachment as death and dying accumulated around them. People became "disease manifestations" to them rather than human beings suffering through nightmares of pain and fear. Norden was aware of the alarming number of medical students, residents, and young practicing physicians who escaped the realities of their profession with drug abuse or suicide, often blaming themselves for any deaths that occurred on their watch.

Norden knew she could not teach people to have compassion, but she could help them learn to express it, to confront their own fears and demons, and to help others with dignity, sympathy, and concern. Her students, she believed, entered medicine because they did care about the suffering of other humans; they simply needed help in handling their own emotions, in knowing how and when to reach out to others, including the families of their patients. As they probed the science and mechanics of the human body, they needed to stop occasionally and realize that the person in the hospital bed was not just a challenging health case but a human being with fears, ambitions, anxieties, relatives, and loved ones. They needed to confront their own mortality and the frailties of the human condition, a reality in which people do die, and a profession that must care both for healing and for helping people and their families face the inevitable with dignity and peace.

To confront these challenges, Norden took classes in grief counseling and introduced "personal hours" in her classes. On one of the first personal days, she gave each student three cards and asked them to write an aspiration they have on one card, the name of someone they love on another, and a talent they prize on the third. She then asked the students to put the cards on their desks face down while she walked around the room snatching a few of them and throwing them in the trash to illustrate the realities their patients will often face: a talent, ambition, or loved one gone forever.[11] She talked to the students about appropriate responses to grief and introduced them to some of the concepts and practices of grief counseling. On other days, she invited surviving family members to discuss how physicians treated them while a relative was ill. People brought pictures, home movies, and other memorabilia and shared their encounters with the medical profession during times of extreme stress.

To make room for this personal development in a class in neuroanatomy, she stopped discussing some of the material she had always included in lectures, leaving students to read more outside of class. The omissions did not reduce their learning. They still reported great confidence in answering neurology questions on the National Boards and continued to perform extremely well in the clinical neurology rotation in the third year of medical school. Norden still presented them with demanding case-based examinations that required everything from recall, comprehension, and application to analysis, synthesis, and evaluation, which her students described as the most intellectually demanding exams they faced in medical school. Rather than detracting from what they learned about the structures and operations of the brain, the maladies that can beset it, and appropriate medical responses, the personal sessions gave students a richer context in which to understand and remember the facts, and a compelling incentive to do so.

Norden is not alone in seeing the wisdom of concentrating on both the personal and the intellectual development of her students. An increasing number of medical schools incorporate both aspects into their medical training. On the undergraduate level, we found scientists and humanists who asked their students to confront questions of justice, to unleash the powers of amazement and fascination with the universe, and to focus on both the exercise of ethical behavior and the ability to make judgments from the application of scientific methods. Many of our subjects were interested in the personal development of their students, in probing what it means to be human, in helping their students develop the capacity to exercise compassion, in recognizing the emotional forces that shape students' lives, and in asking the most powerful of moral questions, "What would you have done?"

Jeanette Norden argued that every discipline can find ways "to confront students with questions of who they are as human beings." In a South American history course, she said, the instructor could use the "disappearances" during the military governments in Brazil and Argentina "to get students to confront human responsibilities in the face of such atrocities and what they might do in a similar situation." Some historians believe that the clergy in Brazil kept the numbers lower by condemning the kidnappings. "That's a wonderful opportunity," Norden pointed out, "to ask students what they think about people who take a courageous stand against repression, and whether they could do the same." In an astronomy class, she argued, the professor "could use John Barrows's famous statement that 'every nucleus of carbon in our bodies originated in the stars,' to generate a discussion about how students feel about themselves as a part of the cosmos."

Ann Woodworth and her colleagues in the Theatre Department at Northwestern teach acting as a study of human nature rather than simply as the learning of lines and the staging of productions. They often take a master-class approach that has application in fields as diverse as math and law. For introductory classes, they have developed a series of explorations to help students examine themselves, cultures, and other people, contemplating movements, textures, emotions, rhythm, attitudes, and motivations long before any lines are spoken. Each piece in the sequence is chosen to spark a particular development in the student rather than simply to achieve a specific performance. In class, Woodworth will watch with intensity as one of her students performs some carefully chosen and sequenced exercise, never hinting that she may have experienced something similar a hundred times before.

"Let's see," she will say, once the performance is over. "I think we have something we can work with." Then with a combination of Socratic questions and delicate suggestions, she will begin a conversation with the student as other learners watch (the master-class approach). "Let's do it again, only this time, I want you to think about . . . ," she will say; or after a long pause of intense concentration, she will ask the students a question intended to spark imagination and reconsideration, to get them to explore their own experiences. Sometimes, she will turn to the class and ask for their comments and questions, quietly and slowly taking each student seriously. Because she knows her art and craft, because she and her colleagues have thought so carefully about the abilities students must develop to act and even the sequence in which those abilities and insights might be cultivated, because they have identified in considerable detail where and how students are likely to go wrong in the development of good acting, she is able to guide and prod her students toward magnificent performances and the capacity to understand themselves, how they achieved that higher level, and who they are as human beings. Typically, she does all of that without any sense of judgment. "You must want to do this," she will say, "and be willing to spend the time it takes to develop your character. But the choice is yours." It is a message we heard again and again.

Woodworth's day classes are filled with students of enormous talent, many of them already under contract with agents. Her graduates include some glitzy luminaries from theater, television, and the movies. Students must meet demanding standards to get into Northwestern, and they must prove themselves to stay in the acting program. But when she teaches in the night school, anyone can sign up. Those classes might include a hodgepodge of people, from aging professors and carpenters to retired accountants and departmental assistants. There often isn't much acting experience among them and little chance that they will make a career of it. Whereas many of the day students are headed to highly successful careers and awards on Broadway and in Hollywood, most of the night students will never see that life. Nonetheless, Woodworth takes every person in those night classes just as seriously as she does her day students. She plunges into each exercise with the same vigor, working with people both individually and in groups. She often manages to stimulate some remarkable acting, transforming performances almost like magic. But she also fosters a perspective on human behavior that usually leaves a lasting impression on the way her students view themselves and others.

The teachers we studied all shared this view that learning takes place not when students perform well on examinations but when they evaluate how they think and behave well beyond the classroom. They stressed that the ability merely to reach "correct" answers has little significance if it does not reflect functional understanding. Don Saari, the highly successful math professor at the University of California mentioned earlier, emphasizes the ability to think critically about calculus problems rather than the capacity to "plug and chug" toward some correct solution. The best teachers want to challenge students to think differently, to ask questions that expose problems with the faulty notions students bring into the class, and generally to put them intellectually in situations in which they must question and rebuild their conceptions. They stress the need for students to grapple with important concepts and ideas, to see them from a variety of perspectives, and to build their own understanding of the material.

They believe that students are unlikely to engage in any meaningful learning, to re-examine their thinking in some fundamental way, unless (1) they come to care deeply about issues involved in their thinking—deeply and extensively enough that they are willing to grapple, probe, question, look for reasons, and build coherent conceptual frameworks—and (2) they have ample opportunity to apply their learning to meaningful problems. Thus they ask students to solve intellectual, artistic, practical, physical, and abstract problems that the students find intriguing, beautiful, and important. They often create collaborative environments and both challenge and support their students' efforts, providing them with honest and helpful feedback.

The best teachers ask themselves what they hope students can do intellectually, physically, or emotionally by the end of the course and why those abilities are important. They sometimes discard or place less emphasis on traditional goals in favor of the capacity to comprehend, to use evidence to draw conclusions, to raise important questions, and to understand one's thinking. In most disciplines, that means they emphasize comprehension, reasoning, and brilliant insights over memory, order, punctuality, or the spick-and-span. Spelling, the size of margins or fonts, and the style of footnotes and bibliographies are trivial in comparison to the power to think on paper; conceptual understanding of chemistry is more important than remembering individual details; the capacity to think about one's thinking—to ponder metacognitively—and to correct it in progress is far more worthy than remembering any name, date, or number. The ability to understand the principles of calculus problem-solving and to apply those principles and concepts in thinking critically through a problem outranks any capacity to reach the correct answer on any particular question. These teachers want their students to learn to use a wide range of information, ideas, and concepts logically and consistently to draw meaningful conclusions. They help their students achieve those levels by providing meaningful directions and exemplary feedback that quietly yet forcefully couple lofty ideals with firm confidence in what students can do—without making any judgments of their worth as human beings. Most significant, they help students shift their focus from making the grade to thinking about personal goals of development.

The best teachers we encountered expect "more" from their students. Yet the nature of that "more" must be distinguished from expectations that may be "high" but meaningless, from goals that are simply tied to the course rather than to the kind of thinking and acting expected of critical thinkers. That "more" is, in the hands of teachers who captivate and motivate students and help them reach unusually high levels of accomplishment, grounded in the highest intellectual, artistic, or moral standards, and in the personal goals of the students. We found that the best teachers usually have a strong faith in the ability of students to learn and in the power of a healthy challenge, but they also have an appreciation that excessive anxiety and tension can hinder thinking. Thus, while they help students to feel relaxed and to believe in their capacity to learn, they also foster a kind of disquietude, the feeling that stems from intellectual enthusiasm, curiosity, challenge, and suspense, and from the wonderful promises that they make about what students can achieve.

In a recent article Claude Steele argued that students come to class with a variety of backgrounds too complex to put into one simple category, a reality that called for "rendering unto the right students the right intervention." For example, students who have been victims of negative social images that their group can't do well in school but who still care about their academic performance require much different treatments than those targets of negative stereotypes who have decided to give up. For the former, tutoring could remind them that other people think they are inferior and need help. The latter need protection from stereotype threats, but they also require better skills and social support. They need challenging work rather than simple remediation, and an environment that constantly tells them that intelligence can be expanded. They require what Steele called "nonjudgmental responsiveness," which might include tutors who provide Socratic questioning that doesn't judge, dish out empty praise, or focus on right or wrong answers. Both groups, he argued, require teachers who provide critical feedback and faith in students' potential.[12]

Although the teachers we studied said it differently, they seemed to have grasped the essence of Steele's message: every student requires something special. No single approach can work for everyone. Paul Baker put it this way: "My strongest feeling about teaching is that you must begin with the student. As a teacher you do not begin to teach, thinking of your own ego and what you know . . . The moments of the class must belong to the student—*not the students*, but to the very undivided student. You don't teach a class. You teach a student."[13]

A few years ago, one of my colleagues at Northwestern gave a talk on teaching that she called "Are Lectures Useless?" It was actually a vigorous defense of lectures, but the question mark in the title sent another professor on campus into intellectual apoplexy. Armed with the flyer that announced the event, he strolled into class one day ready to tilt at the windmills in his mind, those evil forces raising doubts about the wisdom of his favorite pedagogical weapon. "I want you to know," he told a slightly bewildered student audience while waving the flyer before them, "the teaching center at this university wants us to believe that lectures are no good, but I'm going to continue to lecture whether they like it or not."

More recently, a professor attended one of our summer institutes, fortified with what she believed to be incontrovertible evidence that no one could learn from something called lectures. As part of the program, we featured a demonstration of what students consider to be an outstanding lecture. Our visitor was horrified that anyone would even consider teaching by telling, and later took the opportunity of an elevator ride with the speaker to deliver a fierce tongue-lashing.

These two episodes are part of a growing national debate about lecturing in class. One side in that squabble is convinced that research has proven that lectures never work; the other is often passionately devoted to using the ancient pedagogical device. While this debate has no doubt opened some minds to the possibilities of using tools other than a formal lecture, it has just as often produced rigid positions that shed little light on good teaching, each side convinced that they know a simple truth. Our study of outstanding teachers revealed, however, that some people can engage their students with good lectures, helping and encouraging them to learn on the highest level; others can do so with case studies, problem-based learning, powerful assignments, playing guide by the side, conducting discussions, or creating stimulating field work. Yet any of these methods can also fail miserably.

So what distinguishes the successful from the unsuccessful? First, some underlying principles cut across practices and shape the learning environment, whether a teacher lectures or not. Second, a few key techniques propel the application of those principles. To understand what makes teaching successful, we must explore both principles and techniques.

UNIFYING PRINCIPLES

Seven fairly common principles emerged in the practices of the teachers we studied.

1. Create a Natural Critical Learning Environment

More than anything else, the best teachers try to create a natural critical learning environment: "natural" because students encounter the skills, habits, attitudes, and information they are trying to learn embedded in questions and tasks they find fascinating—authentic tasks that arouse curiosity and become intrinsically interesting; "critical" because students learn to think critically, to reason from evidence, to examine the quality of their reasoning using a variety of intellectual standards, to make improvements while thinking, and to ask probing and insightful questions about the thinking of other people.

Some teachers create this environment within lectures; others, with discussions; and still others, with case studies, role playing, field work, or a variety of other techniques. A few create it with a central project that students take on, often working collaboratively

with other members of the class. Sometimes students tackle the
problems silently while hearing them raised in provocative lectures
designed to offer them ideas and evidence that challenge their previous ways of thinking. Other times, they address the problems in
small groups or in larger class discussions. Indeed, the method
of choice varies considerably depending on a variety of factors,
including the learning objectives, the personality and cultures of
teachers and students, and the learning habits of both. But the
method matters far less than do the challenge and permission for
students to tackle authentic and intriguing questions and tasks, to
make decisions, to defend their choices, to come up short, to receive
feedback on their efforts, and to try again. The best teaching creates
a sense that everyone is working together, whether that means
working on a problem silently while listening to the professor or
reasoning aloud with other students and the professor. Moreover,
the questions, issues, and problems are authentic: they seem important to students and are similar to those that professionals in the
field might undertake.[1]

An intriguing question or problem is the first of five essential
elements that make up the natural critical learning environment.
The second crucial element is guidance in helping the students
understand the significance of the question. Some teachers accomplish this by framing the question in such a way that its implications are clear, giving it power and provocation. Several years ago,
we asked Robert Solomon, a philosophy professor from the University of Texas, to talk about his teaching to a group of faculty members. Solomon called his talk "Who Killed Socrates?" and in that
title captured much of the intellectual energy of his inquiry into
Socratic pedagogy and why it isn't used much anymore. When we
watched Solomon conduct an introductory philosophy class on
epistemology, he simply stood before the group of freshmen and
sophomores, looked them in the eye, and asked, "Does anyone here
know *anything* for sure?" The way he asked the question gave it

meaning. Because people learn most effectively when they are trying to answer their own questions, Solomon's effort helped his students accept his inquiries as their own. As students cast about for a
positive answer, reeling in one solution and then another, they
began to grasp the purpose of this modern inquiry. Once that happened, their learning could begin.

Many teachers never raise questions; they simply give students
answers. If they do tackle intellectual problems, they often focus
only on their subject and the issues that animate the most sophisticated scholarship in the field. In contrast, the best teachers tend to
embed the discipline's issues in broader concerns, often taking an
interdisciplinary approach to problems. When Dudley Herschbach
teaches chemistry at Harvard, he does so with a combination of science, history, and poetry, telling stories about human quests to
understand the mysteries of nature. Because he regards science as a
journey rather than a set of facts, he takes his students into the historical struggle to fathom the universe. The lesson on polymers
becomes the story of how the development of nylons influenced the
outcome of World War II. He invokes the arts, using them to capture the emotional power and beauty with which the poet or the
painter stirs the imagination and wonder. He even asks his chemistry students to write poetry while they struggle to comprehend
the concepts and ideas that scientists have developed.

Often the most successful questions are highly provocative, what
one person outside the study derisively called "come-on" questions. What would you do if you came home from college and found
your father dead and your mother married to your uncle, and the
ghost of your father appeared saying that he had been murdered?
Why did some societies get in boats and go bother other people
while others stayed at home and tended to their own affairs? Why
are human beings occasionally willing to leave home and hearth and
march off into the wilderness, desert, or jungle and kill each other
in large numbers? Why are some people poor and other people rich?

How does your brain work? What is the chemistry of life? Can people improve their basic intelligence?

Sometimes teachers tell a story or remind students how the current question relates to some larger issue that already interests them. When Solomon taught an advanced undergraduate course in existentialism, he began with a story about life under Nazi rule in occupied France in the early 1940s, reminding students that even ordinary activities like whispering to a friend could have dire consequences in that police state. He used that account both to help students understand the political and social conditions that shaped Sartre's thinking and to raise questions about the origins and meaning of existentialism.

Third, the natural critical learning environment also engages students in some higher-order intellectual activity: encouraging them to compare, apply, evaluate, analyze, and synthesize, but never only to listen and remember. Often that means asking students to make and defend judgments and then providing them with some basis for making the decision. They might judge the argument they encounter on some important question, decide when and how to use a certain method, determine the implications of what they encounter, or make choices between different methods of solving a problem. Or do all of these. Robert Divine raises an important question about U.S. history, helps students see that question in the context of larger issues, shares with them briefly some of the ways that other scholars have attempted to answer that question, then challenges the class to evaluate the argument he would make. Donald Saari uses a combination of stories and questions to challenge students to think critically about calculus. "When I finish this process," he explained, "I want the students to feel like they have invented calculus and that only some accident of birth kept them from beating Newton to the punch." In essence, he provokes them into inventing ways to find the area under the curve, breaking the process into the smallest concepts (not steps) and raising the questions that will Socratically pull them through the most difficult moments. Unlike so many in his discipline, he does not simply perform calculus in front of the students; rather, he raises the questions that will help them reason through the process, to see the nature of the questions and to think about how to answer them. "I want my students to construct their own understanding," he explains, "so they can tell a story about how to solve the problem."

Fourth, that environment also helps students answer the question. Some of the professors we studied raised important inquires but challenged students to develop their own explanations and understanding—and defend them. "My greatest success comes," Saari said about his calculus classes, "when I get students to answer the questions for themselves." Others advanced arguments and explanations to aid that process, even sometimes using a "lecture" to do so.

Fifth, the natural critical learning environment leaves students with a question: "What's the next question?" "What can we ask now?" Some instructors respond to questions with a question: "What do *you* think?" "If this is true, then why (how, what, where, etc.) . . . ?" "What do you mean by that?" A few of the teachers we studied used a technique that we first encountered in the 1960s, but that has probably been around much longer than that. At the end of class, they would often ask students two questions: "What major conclusions did you draw?" "What questions remain in your mind?" (In the 1980s a few educators discovered this routine, gave it various names—one-minute paper, immediate feedback, and so forth—and claimed it as their own.) Sometimes they would ask students why they drew the conclusions they did. They might raise this question in open discussions or ask students to provide a written response. With the advent of the Internet, some instructors ask for responses on-line after class.

Depending on the teacher, these five elements appeared in interactive lectures or emerged in discussions or problem-based sessions.

In the 1990s, the Institute for the Learning Sciences at Northwestern worked with several professors to develop highly interactive multimedia programs that tried to create the natural critical learning environment. Larry Silver, a professor of art history at the University of Pennsylvania, for example, developed software called "Is It a Rembrandt?" In that program, a museum curator confronts students with this problem: A prestigious exhibit of Rembrandt's work is about to open, but some questions have emerged about the authenticity of three of the paintings. Each student becomes the museum's top art investigator to look into the suspicions. To do so, the students must examine the paintings and build a case to support their conclusions. They can inspect each piece of art, compare it to similar works, view the curator's files, or go to the conservation lab. At each turn, they encounter questions, but they decide which ones to pursue, picking their own path through the material. If they decide to inspect a painting, for example, they can select an area to view in detail, asking about brushwork and composition. They can ask questions about other works and their relationship to the art they are investigating. An art expert pops up on the screen to provide a short answer, and each answer produces more questions. When, for example, the students have been drawn into a close examination of the brushwork on the face of the painting *Old Man with a Gorgat*, they can ask whether Rembrandt's students also mixed brushwork styles in their paintings. If they do ask, Professor Silver appears to tell them about "bravura display," and the students can then ask, "What is bravura brush stroke?" something that would never have been asked except in this context.

Slowly, the students build their understanding of art history, the important questions that the discipline pursues, and what constitutes evidence to answer those inquiries. They develop an understanding of the art world in which Rembrandt worked and of the community of critics, connoisseurs, collectors, scholars, and controversies that have emerged over the years around the work of the

Dutch master, his students, and his imitators. They build a vocabulary for thinking about various issues, a knowledge and understanding of technical details and procedures, and an ability both to remember and to use a vast array of historical facts. In short, they learn to think like a good art historian, to understand and appreciate the questions that the discipline pursues, to frame important questions of their own, and to understand the kinds of evidence that might help resolve controversies and how to use that evidence to do so. And they do all that while building their case about how to attribute certain paintings rather than simply trying to commit facts to memory.

When the students think they can make a case for a particular conclusion, they marshal their evidence and present it to the museum curator. If the argument is weak, she responds with constructive criticism, sending the students back to the investigation. Even if the case is strong, new questions always remain. Any conclusion simply opens other areas of possible investigation.

Gerald Mead developed a similar program for his course on the history of modern France called "Invitation to a Revolution," which invites students to travel to the late eighteenth century to see if they can avoid the excesses of the French Revolution. In Deborah Brown's physics course, students can use a program that challenges them to build an elevator. In Jean Goodwin's course on free speech, students can act as Supreme Court justices to decide a tricky but actual case that asks whether people can be held legally responsible for the long-range consequences of their speech. In still another program called "Emerging Economies," management students can advise the CEO of a fictitious company on how to do business in an emerging economy.

The power of these programs lies not in their sophisticated computer programming (indeed, one might even argue that they would work more effectively outside the "box") but in the creation of natural critical learning environments in which students can learn by doing, by confronting tasks, intellectual or otherwise, that they want to do.

Fascinating? Yes, but enormously expensive to create. Yet we saw the same kind of natural critical learning environments created in classes that used simulations, case studies, problems, field work, and even lectures. We saw them when Chad Richardson's students did ethnographic research on their own cultures, and when Charlie Cannon's students struggled with how to treat pollution in New York Harbor. Ed Muir, a professor of Italian Renaissance history, recreates trials from that era to help students develop both an understanding of the period and how to use evidence to draw historical conclusions. Donald Saari takes a roll of toilet paper into class, asks students how they will calculate its volume, then nudges them toward breaking that problem into its simplest components. Jeanette Norden confronts her students with actual people who have suffered some malady and challenges the future physicians to think through real clinical cases. Some instructors use case studies. In a history class, for example, students might work in groups to represent various historic interests. In an international relations class, they might formulate policy for Richard Nixon when Salvador Allende, a Marxist, was elected president of Chile in 1970, and later in that same hour, advise Allende—from the perspective of 1972—on how to respond to the economic warfare that the Nixon administration had waged over the previous two years. To prepare for any of these cases, students must work in groups to research the events and the factions they represent, reading a variety of historical accounts and documents. In the process, they learn to recognize the nature of historical questions and how to use evidence to help resolve them. They explore conflicting interpretations and how they might begin to evaluate them, using the evidence, concepts, and reasoning of the discipline.

I have stressed in this chapter that the natural critical learning environment is not dependent on whether or not teachers lecture. But lectures from highly effective teachers nearly always have the same five elements of natural critical learning noted above. They begin with a question (sometimes embedded in a story), continue with some attempt to help students understand the significance of the question (connecting it to larger questions, raising it in provocative ways, noting its implications), stimulate students to engage the question critically, make an argument about how to answer that question (complete with evidence, reasoning, and conclusion), and end with questions. The only exception? Sometimes the best teachers leave out their own answers whereas less successful lecturers often include only that element, an answer to a question that no one has raised.

In the hands of the most effective instructors, the lecture then becomes a way to clarify and simplify complex material while engaging important and challenging questions, or to inspire attention to important matters, to provoke, to focus. It is not used as an encyclopedic coverage of some subject, or as a way to impress students with how much the teacher knows. We found no great teachers who relied solely on lectures, not even highly gifted ones like Jeanette Norden, but we did find people whose lectures helped students learn deeply and extensively because they raised questions and won students' attention to those issues. The students became engaged in thinking through the problems, in confronting them, in looking at evidence, and in reasoning rather than memorizing. Most important, the lecture was part of a larger quest, one element of a learning environment rather than the entire experience.

Some people use highly interactive lectures in which they might occasionally stop and ask students to talk about a topic, to discuss their understanding, or to consider when and how some concept or procedure might be applied. Many of them organize the class into small groups and carefully craft assignments to charge those groups with working collaboratively outside of class to confront the intellectual problems and questions of the course. With some topics they might give students a written "lecture" to read in class, asking them to identify its central arguments and conclusions. Because students can read in fifteen minutes what it takes fifty minutes to say in a lecture, they could then gather in their groups to discuss for another fifteen minutes the meaning, application, implications, and so forth of the material in the "lecture." In the final twenty minutes the instructor can entertain questions, clarify misunderstandings, suggest how students can learn more, ask additional questions, summarize, and finally ask students to write their major conclusions and why they drew those conclusions. In some disciplines, the instruction might begin the last twenty minutes when the teacher asks one or more groups to offer a brief summary of the central argument and major conclusion of the "lecture" or, in other fields, to go to the board and work a problem by applying the methods covered in the written material.[2]

One teacher often asks students to play the devil's advocate and submit every argument they can imagine against the conclusions he draws in class. In recent years he has asked them to submit their responses on-line. Another instructor asks students to list assumptions that she and other scholars are making in reaching certain conclusions. Still another occasionally asks students to discuss the implications of central conclusions or principles.

In all these examples of natural critical learning environments, students encounter safe yet challenging conditions in which they can try, fail, receive feedback, and try again without facing a summative evaluation. They learn by doing and even by failing. They gain specific reasoning skills while the experience itself tells them and their teacher if they have learned to reason in the discipline.

A simple yet profound perception guides the natural critical learning experience: People tend to learn most effectively (in ways that make a sustained, substantial, and positive influence on the way they act, think, or feel) when (1) they are trying to solve problems (intellectual, physical, artistic, practical, or abstract) that they find intriguing, beautiful, or important; (2) they are able to do so in a challenging yet supportive environment in which they can feel a sense of control over their own education; (3) they can work collaboratively with other learners to grapple with the problems; (4) they believe that their work will be considered fairly and honestly; and (5) they can try, fail, and receive feedback from expert learners in advance of and separate from any judgment of their efforts.

2. Get Their Attention and Keep It

Whereas the ideas of natural critical learning serve as a robust organizing rationale around which the best teaching takes place, some more specific principles guide the actions of the people we studied. They consciously try to get students' attention with some provocative act, question, or statement. "The human mind must first focus on the problem of how to understand, apply, analyze, synthesize, or evaluate something," one of the professors told us in an argument we heard frequently, "and a teacher can help stimulate that focus." Teaching is "above all," Michael Sandel, a Harvard political theorist, argued, "about commanding attention and holding it." That means not just generally motivating students' interest in the subject but capturing and keeping their attention for each class. "Our task," Sandel contended, "is not unlike that of a commercial for a soft drink or any other product." The only difference, he went on to argue, is what professors might do with that attention once they catch it. "For the most part," he said, "we want to hold the attention of students for the sake of changing the things they are likely to pay attention to most of the time. We want to grasp students and direct their attention some place else."

Teachers succeed in grabbing students' attention by beginning a lecture with a provocative question or problem that raises issues in ways that students had never thought about before, or by using stimulating case studies or goal-based scenarios.

3. Start with the Students Rather Than the Discipline

To gain students' attention and hold it for some higher purpose, the best teachers start with something that, as Sandel put it, "students care about, know, or think they know, rather than just lay out a blueprint or an outline or tale or theory or account of our own." Several ideas rest at the heart of this approach. For Sandel and many others, the method is grounded in Socratic dialogues. "Socrates began," Sandel explains, "by attending to what people thought they knew, and then he tried gradually and systematically to wrench them from their familiar place." Such an approach often means asking students to begin struggling with an issue from their own perspective even before they know much about it, getting them to articulate a position. Donald Saari does some of that when he gets students to break a calculus problem into smaller pieces. Using Socratic questioning, he begins with what "common sense" might suggest to the students; then, through additional probing, he helps them add the "muscle" that disciplinary discoveries can give them. Sandel compares this method of teaching to ways that he might teach one of his children to play baseball: "I could give them detailed instructions on how to hold the bat, where to stand, how to look for the ball from the pitcher, and how to swing, never letting them hold a bat until they had heard several lectures on the subject. Or, I could give them a bat and allow them to take a few swings, after which I might find one thing that the kid is doing, which if adjusted, would make him a better hitter." The second approach seems eminently more sensible than the first for teaching someone baseball, and it is the method Sandel and others use to teach students to think.

Every year more than seven hundred students crowd into Sandel's classroom at Harvard to take his course on justice. To help them become good political philosophers, he introduces on the first day of class an intriguing puzzle that raises many of the questions with which he wants students to grapple. He asks them to imagine the following scenario: You are the driver of a runaway trolley car that is approaching five men who are working on the track. You cannot stop the train, and it seems destined to run over the men and kill them. As you speed down the track toward this waiting tragedy, you notice a side track where you can steer the trolley car if you choose to do so. The only problem is that one man is working on that track and the train will undoubtedly kill him if it goes that way. What would you choose to do, he asks the students? Do you turn the car onto the side track, killing one person but saving five others? What would be most just and why? Often the students have no difficulty deciding that they would take out the one life to save the five others.

Sandel then introduces a wrinkle to the story. Suppose, he says, that you are not on the train but standing on an overpass watching it speed toward the five workers. As you watch this disaster in the making, you notice a large man standing next to you, also peering over the railing of the overpass. You quickly calculate that if you push this person over the railing, he will land on the track in front of the train. He will die, but his body will stop the train, saving five lives. Would it be just to give that person a shove?

In that exercise Sandel hopes to provoke students to think about fundamental issues of justice and understand their own thinking in relationship to that of some of the major philosophers. When they start, they may be no more prepared for their task than his sandlot kids are to play in the big leagues, but they learn by doing and receiving feedback on their efforts. Throughout the course, Sandel then embeds all the major philosophical schools and writers he wishes to consider in contemporary ideological battles intended to excite the students. His knowledge of the history of ideas helps him select the proper passage from Mills or Kant; his knowledge of and concern for the students helps him select the political, social, and moral debates that will engage them. Equally important, he constantly changes the issues to fit new generations of students.

Many of the best teachers make a deliberate and carefully measured effort to confront some paradigm or mental model that students are likely to bring with them to class. That practice too breaks with convention. Most customary instruction follows an organization that stems wholly from the discipline, a set of topics and subjects that need to be taught—or covered. The approach we encountered in our study takes into consideration both the discipline and student learning, asking what important troublesome (from the discipline's perspective) notions students are likely to hold and then designing instruction that challenges each one progressively, picking the order that will best help students to develop an integrated understanding of the whole. We saw entire classes organized around a series of mental models that the students were likely to bring with them that the course wished to challenge. Such courses were powerful models of what can be called "student-centered" rather than "discipline-" or "teacher-centered" education.

This idea of beginning where the students are rather than where disciplinary traditions might dictate has another influence on practices in the classroom: It leads to explanations that start with the simple and move toward the more complex. "If students have an understanding that is down here," Jeanette Norden explained, putting her hand close to the floor, "you don't start with something up here. Some medical students come in not even knowing what a neuron is—a neuron is a cell in the brain—so you have to begin with that simple notion and then you can build from there quickly."[3]

4. Seek Commitments

Exceptional teachers ask their students for a commitment to the class and the learning. Some people do so in first-day exercises that lay out the promises and plans of the course. They ask students to decide if they really want to pursue the learning objectives in the manner described. Others spell out specific obligations they see as part of the decision to join the class. "I tell my students the first day of class that the decision to take the class is the decision to attend the class every time it meets," one professor explained. "I also tell them that my decision to teach the class includes the commitment to offer sessions worth attending, and I ask them to let me know if they think I'm not doing that." Donald Saari, the math professor, and Richard Leuptow, an award-winning engineer, exact such dedications from their students. That's what Charlie Cannon is doing when he lays out the project and the collaborative responsibilities the first day of his innovation studio. With a firm but friendly request, Leuptow asks his students for a show of hands that they are willing to be on time for every class and participate intellectually in the deliberation of each day. "The decision to take the course is yours," we heard more than one person say, "but once you make that decision, you have responsibilities to everyone else in this community of learners."

There is a subtle but extremely important difference between this approach and that of professors who try to rule like drill sergeants. The teachers in the study never tried to command students; instead, they asked for their commitment *if* they planned to take the class. "I want my students to decide whether they really want to take this class, to pursue these goals," a professor told us, "and to realize what is entailed in that pursuit within this class. I ask them to think about it and decide." Even without any formal and public ceremonies of commitment, highly effective teachers approach each class as if they expect students to listen, think, and respond. That expectation appears in scores of little habits: the eye contact they make, the enthusiasm in their voice, the willingness to call on students. It contrasts sharply with professors who seldom if ever look at their students, who continue on in some set piece almost as if they do not expect students to listen, and who never try to generate a discussion or ask for a response because they don't expect anyone to have any.

5. Help Students Learn outside of Class

The professors do in class what they think will best help and encourage their students to learn outside of class, between one meeting and the next. That approach is fundamentally different from simply deciding to do something because it is traditional or because it "deals with" or "covers" some subject, but it might lead to a variety of orthodox approaches: an explanation that helps to clarify and simplify, enabling students to read or study more complex material; a discussion that gives students a chance to confront new questions and explore their own thinking with others before tackling a project; a demonstration that both confronts existing notions and provokes confrontation with new ones; a debate that enables students to practice critical thinking and to realize gaps in their own understanding and reasoning abilities; group work that asks students to grapple together and helps build a sense of community. The difference comes in the planning and in why teachers make their choices. Because the best teachers plan their courses backward, deciding what students should be able to do by the end of the semester, they map a series of intellectual developments through the course, with the goal of encouraging students to learn on their own, engaging them in deep thinking. In ordinary classes, instructors might create assignments for students, but they rarely use the class to help students do the work.

6. Engage Students in Disciplinary Thinking

The most effective teachers use class time to help students think about information and ideas the way scholars in the discipline do.

They think about their own thinking and make students explicitly aware of that process, constantly prodding them to do the same. They do not think only in terms of teaching their discipline; they think about teaching *students* to understand, apply, analyze, synthesize, and evaluate evidence and conclusions. Some use a Socratic method; others accomplish much the same end with a combination of explanations and questions. "We cannot learn to reason without something to reason about," one teacher told us, "but knowledge comes not through rote memorization of isolated facts, but from the ability to reason, that is, the ability to draw conclusions from reason." We saw instructors call attention to specific reasoning as they made explanations or conducted a discussion. We saw professors constantly asking students to analyze the arguments they encounter in lectures, readings, and from each other. On examinations, they asked students to use their clinical or scientific or historical reasoning skills, reinforcing the centrality of those abilities in the educational goals for the course.

Through such an approach teachers help students build an understanding of concepts rather than simply perform their discipline in front of them. Unlike many mathematicians, chemists, and economists who spend most of the class time working problems on the board, exceptional teachers from those disciplines offer explanations, analogies, and questions that will help students understand fundamental concepts and consequently solve their own problems. While others argue that students must learn (memorize?) information first and use reasoning only later, the professors we studied assume that learning facts can occur only when students are simultaneously engaged in reasoning about those facts.

In class, they might engage students in a highly interactive "lecture" in which they present a problem and coax students into identifying the kinds of evidence they would need to consider to solve that problem and how that evidence might be gathered: "Here's the evidence we've encountered thus far; what do you make of it? What problems do you see? What questions would you ask about this evidence? What evidence do we need to answer those questions, and how will we find or collect that evidence? Here are some results of doing what you suggested. Now, what are the questions, the kind of evidence, and tentative conclusions (hypotheses)?" Others might ask students to work in groups to identify central arguments, the kinds of evidence (observed or inferred) contained in the argument, the types of agreements and disagreements that exist between two arguments (belief and attitude), the assumptions and implications of the arguments, and the appropriate lines of additional inquiry.

7. Create Diverse Learning Experiences

"The brain loves diversity," Jeanette Norden told us repeatedly. To feed that appetite, she and other outstanding teachers conducted class in a multitude of ways. Sometimes they offered visual information (pictures, diagrams, flow charts, time lines, films, or demonstrations); other times, auditory input (speech or visual symbols of auditory information—written words and mathematical notations). They allowed students to talk things out, to interact with each other; but they also gave them a chance to reflect independently or to hear someone else's explanations. Some material was organized inductively, from facts, data, and experimentation to the general principles and theories; other things, deductively, by applying principles to specific situations. The teachers gave students an opportunity to learn sequentially, a piece at a time; they also gave them space to learn globally, through sudden insights. Some of the learning involved repetition and familiar methods; some, innovation and surprises. The very best teachers offered a balance of the systematic and the messy.

"The great contribution of the learning-styles stuff," one teacher told us, "is that it called attention to the need to diversify. I don't think there's much evidence that most people have exclusive learning styles and can't learn in any way but one, but I do think that we all benefit from variety."

EMPLOYING THE CRAFT OF TEACHING IN THE CLASSROOM

As potent as these seven principles may be, they can still fall flat if the professor doesn't act on them well. Performance in front of students affects how well they learn, and it involves a kind of craft of teaching, techniques, and even physical abilities. Such skills cannot transform teaching that has more fundamental weaknesses, but honing these skills can make good teachers even better. This kind of attention to performance is still "student centered," a focus on details for the sake of student learning.

Let's look at two elements of this craft of teaching: the ability to talk and the ability to get students to talk.

Good Talk

Perhaps the most significant skill the teachers in our study displayed in the classroom, laboratory, studio, or wherever they met with students was the ability to communicate orally in ways that stimulated thought. No scholar would deny the importance of writing well, and certainly good writing involves primarily the capacity to think, but it also entails a certain craft and even considerable attention to small details and rules. In academia, the ability to write well has a special status that oral communication no longer enjoys. For our subjects, however, the capacity to talk well—in brief instructions or in long explanations—remains important, a skill as much worth refining as their own writing.

All the best teachers talked to their students, and the quality of those talks made a significant difference in the success of the teaching. Generally the most accomplished of the teachers had the best ways of explaining things, but all our subjects noticed that

improving their oral skills resulted in more positive learning responses from their students. Here I concentrate on the practices
and insights of the very best communicators, those whose students
raved about their stimulating talk, clear directions, and thorough
explanations.

More than anything else, the most successful communicators
treated anything they said to their students—whether in fifty-
minute lectures or in two-minute explanations—as a conversation
rather than a performance. They interacted with students and
encouraged and allowed them to interact with one another and with
the material. They pulled each person in the room into a dialogue,
offering gestures and body language that conveyed their desire to
reach out to each student. Because they wanted their students to
think and understand, to confront the problems, to learn the intellectual skills, and to engage in a conversation with themselves and
each other, they checked on their students' comprehension as they
talked and made sure that everyone in the room was included in the
discussion.

The most effective teachers might begin a point by looking at
one student then move their eyes from one person to another before
finishing the explanation with someone across the room. In a large
room, they might occasionally talk specifically to people in distant
corners of the room ("Can you hear [or see this] from up there?").
Most of the teachers we studied frequently used rhetorical questions, even if it was no more than to ask, "Does this make sense?"
They watched their students' reactions, read their eyes and other
body language, and adjusted what they said to the enlightened, confused, bewildered, or even bored looks they saw in the classroom.
They learned students' names and called on them. They moved
from behind the podium, or avoided artificial obstructions altogether. They asked for feedback from students, stopped to ask for
questions, and paused for ten seconds at a time, looking at students.
Some teachers often visibly struggled with understanding an idea

or how best to explain it, creating a sense of spontaneous exchange and prompting students to feel a part of that same struggle and a part of the conversation. Others engaged in constant banter with their students, allowing them to ask questions, make comments, and remain active in the dialogue. According to Susan Wiltshire, this kind of teaching was not unlike inviting students into exchanges around the dinner table.

To achieve that sense of conversation, however, the teachers paradoxically paid some attention to the quality of their performances, mindful of the number of students and the size and shape of the room. They did not put on a show like some film or television program that played a fixed script regardless of the reactions it sparked, but neither did they ignore the demands of communicating with all their students in one place. Two hundred students required different levels of energy and projection than did six students sitting around a seminar table—or two people sitting in a living room.

The most effective speakers used conversational tones but projected their voices to include everyone present. They spoke clearly and carefully. They would pause to let important points land. They would not start walking in the middle of an important point, or if they were walking, they would not stop until the point had been made. In a large lecture hall, they made gestures larger than life, even to achieve a small effect; in a seminar, they used small actions to achieve large results. Regardless of the size of the room, they spoke as if they knew and wanted to engage every student, including those in the back row.[4]

Many of the people we studied said they had, at sometime in their careers, practiced enunciating clearly—getting the words out of their mouths—or rehearsed an explanation before a mirror. Others told us they had made conscious efforts to keep themselves from pacing or talking to the board, to eliminate some nervous and distracting tic—perhaps discovered after watching a videotape of themselves teaching—or to look at students in the back row, to gesture toward them, and sometimes to ask them questions. Some teachers told us they had worked on the timbre of their voices, on appropriate gestures, or even on their tendency to slouch and mumble through class.

There was within this conversation/performance a sense of the dramatic, a sense of when to stop talking and let a key idea land. That slight change of pace became the exclamation behind a key point, a trigger for thought, for calculation, or for construction of understanding.[5] Robert Divine knew how to ask a good question in a seminar and then how to wait patiently, even through several minutes of silence, while his students thought about their answers. Sometimes highly effective lecturers will pause ever so slightly following a key point and stand perfectly still; their body language will suggest suspended animation as they work to keep their students' attention focused on the point and to give them time to contemplate it. They know how to make silence loud.

They also know when to change pace. Every ten to twelve minutes, they change the rhythm and content of their delivery, shifting direction or focus, altering activities or subject, punctuating an explanation with stories or questions, ending or beginning an exercise. Some teachers sprinkle in humor; others move from the concrete to the abstract. If they are talking, they stop; if they are silent, they say something.

Yet no catalogue of such abilities and preparations can capture fully the ingredient that made these teachers so effective in reaching their students: a strong intention to help them learn.

This old-fashioned notion of intention, so prominent in the theater, played a powerful role in driving the highly effective to say the right thing in the right way. The best teaching occurred when people came into their classes filled with intentions to stimulate every student's interests, to communicate clearly and effectively, to help everybody understand, to provoke responses, to foster deep thinking, to engage, and to entertain multiple perspectives. Those aims and the feeling that went with them influenced everything the teachers did and how they did it. "When I go into the classroom wanting only to get through the hour or to impress my students with my knowledge," one professor told us, "it affects the class. That's when my teaching fails. I can't explain how or why it makes a difference, but it does."

Many professors told us that in the few minutes before they enter a class, they often sit quietly in their offices trying to capture what they want to help and encourage their students to do that day—and in the days to come. Jeanette Norden told us that before she begins the first class in any semester, she thinks about the awe and excitement she felt the first time anyone explained the brain to her, and she considers how she can help her students achieve that same feeling. Ann Woodworth often talks about a ball of power she imagines coming out of the ground and filling her body and soul with an energy that she carries into the classroom or rehearsal hall. Her descriptions sound like a form of self-hypnosis.

Some people may dismiss such practices as so many shenanigans that get in the way of more important preparation, but we need look no further than the ancient practices and insights of the theater to find the power of understanding and using intentions to affect other people. Teaching is not acting, yet good teachers do expect to affect their audience when they talk: to capture their attention, to inspire, to provoke thoughts and questions. The most effective teachers understand that, and they often consciously investigate their own intentions, slowly defining and molding their ambitions in a process that is both rational and emotional. This practice has all the power of careful analysis, but it also entails the energy of feelings and attitudes that no induction and deduction can achieve. Students feel it and respond accordingly. Many of the students we interviewed talked about "something she does" and told us they "can't explain it," but that certain teaching inspired their efforts. When we compared the people they were talking about with their less successful colleagues, we sometimes found nothing in content or structure that could explain the difference either. But we did find that the most effective teachers generally thought more carefully and extensively about their intentions with students and let those aspirations and attitudes guide them in their teaching.[6]

Warm Language

As powerful as these ideas may be, something else marked the communication of the most effective teachers. For years, we struggled with how to think about those additional qualities until Paul Heinrich of the University of Sydney introduced us to the idea of "warm" and "cool" language. Sometimes when we explain something we talk about it rather than talk through it. We dance around the edge, almost afraid to begin with an explanation. "We could do something like this," Heinrich explained: "There was this story about this little girl and three bears and how she went to their house when they were gone and tasted and tried everything and then they came home and discovered her." That language is cool. It doesn't tell the story and assumes that the listener has either already heard the story or would be bored at its telling. It is, Heinrich argues, "detached, less emotional, less descriptive." In contrast, he goes on to say, we could just tell the story: "Once upon a time, there were three bears and a little girl named Goldilocks." That language is warm. It's involved; it tells the whole story rather than just referring to it. Warm language is "essentially story telling," Heinrich explains. "You begin at the beginning and work your way forward to the conclusion. The conclusion remains unknown, even if anticipated, until the end." Warm language tends to be in the present tense, but "even if the past tense is used, the intent is always to take the listener into the moment and work slowly through it 'from the inside.'"

The best professors tended to use warm language, to be explicit, to be complete, and to tell the story and make the explanation. They would raise powerfully worded questions. They would bring their listeners inside the material. Less accomplished professors, in contrast, often used cool language. They would refer to information as if they were afraid to tell the story, skipping important steps in an explanation almost as if they thought that because they had heard it before they need not tell it again.

This is not to say that good teachers never use cool language. They do, but generally only after their warm language has brought students inside the subject, has involved them intellectually and emotionally. They use cool language to remind, to summarize, and warm language to invite, to stimulate.

Making Explanations

Conversational tones, good intentions, and warm language are all important elements of the craft of good talking, but something else distinguishes the most effective communicators. The best teachers simply know how to make good explanations.[7] It goes without saying that they are clear and thorough and stimulate learning, but how do they achieve those results? To gain some insights into this part of their craft, let's concentrate on explanations of concepts or information, the sort of explaining that often goes into lectures but could also appear in answers to students' questions. In general, exceptional teachers begin with simple generalizations and then move toward both complexity and specificity. They use familiar language before trying to introduce specialized vocabulary.

Someone once videotaped Richard Feynman sitting in a big easy chair, telling a story about going swimming. Imagine, the physicist offered, that you are sitting next to a swimming pool and someone dives in, creating waves in the water. "It is possible," he explained, "that in those waves there's a clue as to what's happening in that pool." It is also possible, Feynman continued, "that some sort of insect . . . with sufficient cleverness could sit in a corner of the pool and could be disturbed by the waves and by the nature of the irregularities and bumping of the waves [and] . . . figure out who jumped in where and when and what's happening all over the pool." In fact, he explained, "that's what we do when we are looking at something. We have this hole in our head called an eye and waves called light enter that opening, sloshing about to give us information."

As Feynman told the story with an almost childlike giddiness, he gradually added more complexity to the tale. Light waves are like the waves in the water but in three dimensions rather than two. It's all "kind of incredible," Feynman exploded, "because when I'm looking at you someone standing to my left can see somebody who's standing at my right." How could that be? "It's easy to think of them as arrows passing each other. But that's not the way it is. Because all it is, is something shaking. It's called the electric field, but we don't have to bother with what it is. It's just like the water height going up and down. And so there's some quantity that is shaking about here, and in a combination of motions that's so elaborate and complicated that the net result is to produce an influence that makes me see you." Feynman gradually wove x-rays, cosmic rays, and infrared and radio waves into his account.[8]

Several factors made this telling such a good example of the kind of approach we found among highly effective teachers. At each level, he emphasized concepts and understanding basic principles, using his "bug in the pool" story to illustrate and provoke. He stressed broad understanding of basic concepts before adding more complexities and even before bothering to name those ideas. We found that other highly effective teachers follow much the same pattern and may even oversimplify initially with some metaphor, analogy, or explanation that helps the novice begin to understand. Later, as the explanations, examples, and evidence continue to grow, the teacher introduces more complexity that may even challenge those early metaphors, analogies, or explanations. "I often begin with an explanation," one of the teachers told us, "that will help students begin to grasp something, to build their conceptions. Later, as we add more information and ideas, they begin to realize that our initial way of thinking was too simplistic and even mislead-ing. But if I started with the more complex way of explaining some-thing, they would never understand it." Notice that her intention is to help students understand, not to impress them with the sophisti-cation of her knowledge.

When I interviewed one of the mathematicians in the study, he asked me if I knew how to define a function. I confessed that my knowledge was a little rusty, and that the definition I remembered memorizing in college didn't spring immediately to mind, some-thing about variables being related to the values of other variables. "But can you explain the basic concept in your own words?" he per-sisted. I stammered and began looking for the nearest exit. At that point, he tossed a pen in my direction, which I instinctively reached out to catch. "How did you catch that?" he asked. "I opened my hand and then closed it around the pen at the right moment." "But how did you know when to open your hand and when to close it?" he pressed. After a little struggling, and some additional question-ing from the mathematician, I stumbled to the conclusion that I predicted where the pen would be by observing its flight. "That's a function," he exploded. "You took information about where it was at this point, this point, and this point, and predicted when it would arrive in your hand." He then turned to the board and wrote a for-mula. "I could have explained it this way, and that's the way it's ordinarily done. But when we do it that way, students just memo-rize formulas or definitions and really don't grasp what's involved in the concept." We found history professors, chemists, sociolo-gists, economists, biologists, and others who followed much the same approach as the mathematician, stimulating students to under-stand an idea in their own words before bothering with its name or some set language that might define it.

Good explanations start with ways to help the learner begin to construct a good understanding; they are not necessarily the most accurate and detailed way of putting something. They start with

simplicity, with the familiar, and gradually add more complexity
and the unknown. They might begin with a metaphor or generalization. Jeanette Norden called the method her "sandwich approach." She would begin with the bread, a good general account
of some basic and fairly broad ideas. Over time, she would gradually add the mayonnaise, meat, lettuce and tomatoes, until the
students had developed a more sophisticated understanding, and
perhaps could even look back at their first understanding and realize its inadequacies. Good explanations come from people who
realize that learners must construct knowledge rather than simply
absorb it.

Getting Students to Talk

Good teachers know how to talk well, but they also can get students
talking. Indeed, we often heard classes buzzing with lively conversations as questions and ideas darted around the room. Yet talk can
be cheap, bull sessions that produce little understanding or debates
that encourage students to "win an argument" rather than find the
truth. The exceptional teachers did not just want to get students
speaking; they wanted them to think and learn how to engage in an
exchange of ideas. "Let's think about why we conduct class discussions," one of them told us. "Surely, we want more than to fill time
or allow students to work out their nervous tensions so they will
more likely listen to us."

According to Erwin Hargrove, a professor of politics at Vanderbilt, class discussions have a broader purpose. "Remember when
you first started teaching," he reminded a group of his colleagues
several years ago. "If you are typical, you most likely told yourself,
'I'm learning more now than ever before.' We conduct class discussions to give our students a little taste of that experience. We ask
them to struggle with their own thinking and understanding on a
subject, to express their ideas to others, and to have their ideas challenged." The teachers we studied thought a good class discussion

could help students focus on important questions, stimulate them to grapple with key issues, help them acquire intellectual excitement, and give them the opportunity to construct their understanding. We came to judge discussions in much the same way. It didn't matter to us how much students talked; we wanted to hear them grappling with important issues, struggling toward a better understanding of key issues, raising critical and original questions.

What produced that kind of conversation? Most important, there was something to discuss that the students regarded as important and that required them to solve problems. The teacher raised questions that the students had come to regard as significant; or, better yet, the students raised those inquiries, often because the teacher had said something or asked them to read or view something that had puzzled, stirred, provoked, intrigued, disturbed, surprised, or even outraged them. Many teachers used stories to stimulate discussion. Often we heard instructors ask for evaluations and recommendations—even in science and math classes. Donald Saari used his sense of humor, love of puzzles, and trust in the students' ability to think to spark an intense conversation about how to calculate the area under the curve. Michael Sandel posed moral dilemmas to raise profound questions about justice. Jeanette Norden put a human face on neurological disorders, or sparked interest in the brain with her own sense of awe over the one organ that "controls who you are and what you do."

The best teachers didn't ask students to discuss readings; they provoked and guided them into discussing ideas, issues, or problems that some article or chapter might help them approach. The students read those pieces not merely to complete an assignment but to prepare for their intellectual struggle. In the discussion, the teachers asked students what they thought about important issues and problems and why. As ideas began to flow, they pressed them for evidence, questioned them about the nature of the evidence, invoked arguments from the resources, encouraged and allowed students to challenge each other, pointed out agreements and disagreements in belief and attitude, and raised appropriate questions. The teachers we studied often chose rooms with moveable chairs. Many professors created permanent small, heterogeneous groups within a larger class and sometimes had those groups work together in class. Some teachers allowed the groups to emerge voluntarily while others spent considerable time creating them, often trying to ensure a balance of advanced and novice learners. Many instructors encouraged students to form groups of three or four, made some group assignments (for example, find and describe an application for this mathematical principle in your field of interest), then found group homes for those few students who did not quickly join one. Others fashioned groups of five to seven people, assigning students on the basis of information collected in survey forms and deliberately trying to maintain a mix of abilities and backgrounds in each one.

Larry Michelsen, an organizational psychologist at the University of Oklahoma, often plays a game that tends to produce heterogeneous communities. If, for example, he wants to create heterogeneity around the number of years of experience in a given area, he asks the student with the most experience in the area to stand some place in the room, the student with the next longest to stand next, the next longest next, and so forth in a line around the room. If he then wants to create, say, six groups, he assigns a number from one to six to each student in the row, moving in order down the line. He then puts all the one's together, the two's together, and so forth. Thus each group consists of people from each of six different places all along the line of experience.

Several factors seemed to make groups work most effectively. Students responded best when they thought of the group as an opportunity to work on authentic problems rather than as an obligation to fulfill a class assignment, and when the experience had some honorific quality rather than even the hint of remediation. In contrast, some teachers failed with groups either because they gave the students work that required them to do little more than look up "right" answers, or because they compelled the students to work together even when they could work more efficiently alone, or both. The best group work led students to grapple with important questions, to reason collectively through perplexing, intriguing, and significant issues, and to brainstorm solutions to fascinating problems.

Most teachers found heterogeneous groupings more satisfactory than homogeneous ones, and created the diversity around issues of experience and proficiency with the material and the reasoning skills it required. Some teachers let students form their own groups because it gave students control over their own education. "I raise complex questions and then give students resources to help them struggle with the issues," one professor in the social sciences told us, "but I also let and even encourage them to divide up the resources. They make reading assignments to each other." We found little support for group papers, but several instructors told us that they ask (or encourage) students to work collaboratively on resources and ideas for their respective projects.

In one powerful use of group work, the professor gives students four introductions that other students have written to papers and tells them that two of these pieces started papers that eventually won honors while two received a B-minus or lower. He asks the students to read the introductions individually and then to work in their groups to determine which is which and *why* they rank them as they do: "Spell out the criteria that caused you to list any given paper as honors or mediocre work."

After fifteen to twenty minutes, he brings the groups together to report their conclusions and reasons and write them on the board. He then shares his rankings and, most important, his criteria, comparing it with the standards and conclusions they have fashioned.

They begin by negotiating their understanding with one another and then with the instructor as they attempt to build their comprehension of the thinking of a learned community they are trying to join.

To get the discussion going, the best teachers usually pose a question and ask students to spend a few minutes collecting their thoughts on paper or otherwise work on the problem individually before talking. They then ask students to share their thoughts (or solutions) with someone sitting nearby ("think then pair"). The students burst into conversation. After a few more minutes, they might ask pairs to pair up ("think/pair/square"). Finally, they bring the entire class together for a full discussion, starting with the ideas already discussed in the smaller venue, calling on one or two groups to report and defend their conclusions ("think/pair/square/share"). We saw this work well in classes as small as 20 or as large as 200. Marcy Towns, a chemistry professor from Indiana, uses this technique to confront students in large classes with problems that stimulate consideration of important concepts. Suhail Hanna uses it with students learning to write. Paul Travis does something similar to raise questions about historical evidence and interpretation.

Some teachers used the approach to prime students for a discussion. Others used it to spark interaction in the middle of a lecture.[9] In large classes, they might use this "think/pair/square/share" technique to create small groups across a huge lecture hall and to spark dozens of small conversations before building the large one.

If the first law of good discussions is to allow students an opportunity to collect their thoughts (perhaps by writing) and to talk with a neighbor before addressing the whole class, the second rule is to get everyone involved early. Arthur McEvoy, who teaches environmental law at the University of Wisconsin, has used what he jokingly refers to as the "McEvoy-minute around." In small discussion classes, he has everyone sit in a circle. He then gives each student one minute to make his or her initial contribution to the discussion.

"The longer my students sit without saying anything," one professor told us, "the harder it is to bring them into the discussion." Don Saari begins his math classes by questioning students who appear "bolder and ready to jump into the fray." Saari says he sizes them up from the way they sit and look. "How would you do this?" he probes, propping his chin on one hand in the pose of Rodin's Thinker. "That way I can convey a silent message that I will wait for their answer," he explains. Over the first few days, he takes note of the shy students in his class of two hundred, the ones who avoid his gaze, looking to the floor or at their books, pulling themselves back into their bodies. "I will gradually try to help those students feel more comfortable," he explains. "I might talk with them casually before class, get to know a little bit about them, before I call on them."

Like Saari, most highly effective teachers do call on their students rather than just waiting for them to enter the discussion. But they do so with care. As Susan Wiltshire characterized it, they call on people the way they might do so around the dinner table rather than the way they might cross-exam them in a courtroom or challenge them to a duel. Saari's relaxed and humorous style—he is constantly smiling and has a big twinkle in his eye—helps diffuse anxiety. His Thinker pose, his sense of adventure and playfulness, and his reluctance to judge all create a mood of non-judgmental problem-solving. Students generally don't fear being wrong because everyone is wrong at some point as they collectively struggle to understand, and because they know Saari emphasizes understanding over reaching correct answers. "I tell students that it's largely a matter of common sense bolstered by the power of the discipline," he explains. "That encourages them to think, to struggle with ways they might figure out to solve a problem."

In contrast, many less successful teachers play a game that might be called "guess what's on my mind." In that game, there is only one right answer. Some students play it well while others cringe, fearing they might get it wrong and often refusing to contribute.

Ultimately, discussions work well both because the students feel comfortable with one another and the instructor and because the conversation is part of a larger attempt to create what I earlier called a natural critical learning environment. I have already noted that the outline of good lectures contained all the five elements of that environment. It should come as no surprise that the structure of good discussions followed much the same contours. Let's look, for example, at the kind of questions that emerged in case studies or problem-based learning classes.

The best case teachers begin by asking questions such as, What is the key problem we face here? What are we trying to solve? (perhaps using the "write before you talk; talk in small groups before conversing in larger ones" approach). They continue by asking what key facts in this case or that should be used to solve the problem. What do we need to know that we don't know? What are the key definitions and concepts? They might first call on one student, wait for that explanation, and then ask another to summarize what the first person said.

After using such exploratory questions to confront students with a common problem (of understanding, application, analysis, or synthesis) and helping them understand its significance, the best teachers begin to provoke imagination. Are there any good solutions? What are the possibilities? At this level, the instructor might hear wildly conflicting approaches and even ideas that fly in the face of the best scientific and scholarly ideas on the subject (in other words, the students might be wrong!), but they also hear what the students were thinking. Perhaps most important, they get the students to lay their thinking on the table so they can all examine it more closely.

Next, they stimulate some evaluation of those ideas. What solutions (ideas) have we considered? How do we compare solutions? What are the implications of accepting this interpretation, solution, or approach? What are the consequences of doing so? Can you draw even tentative conclusions? Which is the best solution (idea)? Why? What do you reject? Why?

Finally, the best teachers ask concluding questions: What have we learned here? What else do we need to know to confirm or reject our hypothesis? What are the implications of our conclusions? What questions remain unanswered? How do we answer those questions?

We saw professors in a variety of disciplines and circumstances use this pattern or some variation of it. Sometimes the conversation centered around a case study; other times, a problem, a set of readings that raised some significant issue, a lecture, or even an experiment or experience that all the students had encountered. In some fields, the issues were often conceptual ones (how best to understand this development) or questions of interpretation (what does this text mean and what implications does it have for the larger issue at hand?). In other areas, the problems might be about causes or consequences (in history, for example), while in still other disciplines they were more clinical and applied (in medicine and engineering, for example).

Some of the teachers we studied used this pattern quite formally in generating discussions while others appeared more casual. Samuel LeBaron, a physician who teaches at the Stanford University medical school, for example, believes that students will often learn to think more clearly in informal circumstances than they will when they are playing students. He has found the phrase, "before we get started" a powerful way to create those extramural circumstances in which he can raise many of the kinds of questions discussed above. In a lesson on back pain, for example, he walked into the room and told the students, "Before we get started with the lesson, I've been having these back pains and I just can't get rid of them." With a little complaining on his part, the students began to offer him suggestions while he quietly pressed them for explanations and reasons for their thinking, sometimes subtly challenging a line of thinking with what appeared to be a casual question. Yet in that informal atmosphere he carried students from exploratory questions through inquiries about evidence to judgments and their implications.

Of course, no one has achieved great teaching with only vigorous vocal tones, a powerful microphone, good posture, honorable intentions, and strong eye contact—as helpful as they may be. One teacher encouraged us to think about "the relationship between a well-built house and a good paint job." The foundations of that structure, its basic design, and its overall construction determine the qualities of the home. Great teachers are not simply great speakers or discussion leaders; they are, more fundamentally, special kinds of scholars and thinkers, leading intellectual lives that focus on learning, both theirs and their students'. Their attention to the details of performance stems from a concern for the learners, and their focus is on the nature and processes of learning rather than on the performance of the instructor.

HOW DO THEY TREAT
THEIR STUDENTS?

A math professor in our study had a student who was having trouble with calculus—or so it seemed. The student actually did fairly well on small quizzes but performed miserably on each major examination. Nevertheless, he didn't give up. Instead, he attended extra sessions, met with his colleagues in small groups to work on problems, and gave every sign he wanted to learn. Nothing seemed to work, however. He flunked all the big tests. By the end of the course it seemed increasingly apparent that he suffered from an awful case of test anxiety.

At the end of the term, the students faced a comprehensive departmental final that the professor had no hand in preparing. A day before the final, the young man stopped by to see the professor, who started talking about calculus with him, at first casually and then gradually more rigorously. "Do you understand this?" he began asking him, and the student would reply each time that he did. The professor then asked him to explain it. After a while he had the student at the board in his office explaining concepts and working through some fairly difficult problems. In all, the teacher spent nearly two hours reviewing calculus with this young man, asking questions and letting him do most of the thinking and talking. Clearly, the student understood far more about calculus than his grades on the major examinations indicated.

After two hours of work, the professor looked at him and said, "You've just taken an oral examination in calculus. I can't tell you what grade you made just yet. I'll have to think about that, but you have at least passed the course." The student asked him what he should do about the departmental final the next day. "Oh, I don't know. Why don't you go take it just for grins," came the rather offhanded reply. The student did just that, and not only did he pass; he made a B+.

That same professor once had a young woman come to his office early in the term to ask him to sign a drop slip. "Oh, you can't drop," he told her with a mischievous smile, "because we don't allow good students out of the class." When she protested that she was not a good student, the professor began asking her what troubled her about calculus, and for the next hour he talked with her about her difficulties. Patiently and meticulously, he played Socrates, asking her questions that helped her build her own understanding of key concepts and pulling her through difficult points on this intellectual journey. When he finished, she agreed to stay in the class, although she remained a little uneasy. Over the next few class sessions, however, the professor continued to nurture her confidence. Her performance on subsequent quizzes and examinations improved considerably. When she took the departmental final, she made a perfect score and received an A in the course.

We heard a host of such stories from the students of outstanding professors, tales of dedicated educators who did something special. We could easily characterize these acts as pure kindness and suggest that exceptional teachers are simply compassionate people who really care about their students, but that wouldn't tell us much. Besides, it might even be misleading, suggesting that other faculty members don't care. To be sure, we found some professors who had no concern for the welfare and education of the people who took their classes, but many other less successful instructors certainly did, yet their treatment of their students was different—and less effective. Is there something in the way the best professors view and treat their students that might help explain their success?

Before answering that question, just a word about what we didn't find. Despite some popular beliefs to the contrary, personality played little or no role in successful teaching. We encountered both the bashful and the bold, the restrained and the histrionic. A handful of the subjects played aggressive devil's advocates, avoiding the hostility and terror to be sure but nevertheless acting quite assertive. Most of them, however, played more subdued and noncombative roles. Some teachers treated their students quite formally while others broke down virtually all the conventional social barriers between teacher and learner. We found no pattern in instructors' sartorial habits, or in what students and professors called each other. In some classrooms first names were common; in others, only titles and surnames prevailed.

Yet we did find an elaborate pattern of beliefs, attitudes, conceptions, and perceptions behind the way outstanding teachers treated the people who took their classes. The patterns alone couldn't transform otherwise ineffective teaching, but the most effective instructors as a group always came closer to following them than did even their slightly less effective colleagues.

Perhaps the best way to introduce these patterns is to contrast them with the attitudes and behaviors of some professors we ultimately rejected for the study because the learning in their classes was not so impressive. Let's consider, for example, a composite picture of some of those people and call that amalgamation Dr. Wolf. Some of these teachers were men, others were women. To emphasize that neither sex has a monopoly on such behavior, attitudes, and concepts, I use both gender pronouns alternately in the following account.

In each case, we had heard some good things about Professor Wolf and had begun to collect information about his or her teaching. A few students called his class "brilliant" and said it had changed the way they thought about the subject, stimulating them to intellectual insights they had not imagined possible. Yet when we looked closely at the student ratings from Professor Wolf's classes, we found a disturbing pattern. In nearly every class, anywhere from 20 to 50 percent of the students gave him the lowest ratings possible. That by itself would not necessarily cause alarm, but when we began to hear from those students who ranked him so low, they were clearly angry and frustrated.

It would be easy to dismiss such complaints as the carping of students who were not really serious about their studies and who were simply mad because Dr. Wolf didn't give them a free ride. But that didn't appear to be the case. Many of her detractors had excellent academic records and reputations for hard work. As we continued to probe, we began to find something more troubling. One person after another said she was arrogant, did not care about students, ridiculed some people in class, often bragged about the high numbers who flunked her course, and set harsh and arbitrary demands. Even some who praised her work told us that she abused others in the class.

In one account after another, one theme began to emerge consistently. Dr. Wolf was, as one person put it, "a control freak" who wanted to let his students know how much he knew, how little they knew, and how much power he had over their lives. "He wants to control everything," someone told us, and he "will put down anyone he sees as a threat."

In class, the professor was reluctant to answer questions. Her most interactive moments with students were always combative; she would take a question as an opportunity to duel with someone intellectually until she had won the battle. She was particularly fond of drawing her students in one direction before leaving them out to dry with some carefully planned pontification to the contrary. Everything seemed to revolve around her needs, including the desire, as one student put it, "to be the star of the show."

Students had similar views of the way Dr. Wolf offered criticism or feedback on their efforts. "I felt like I had been judged and put away," one person reported. "He seemed to take delight in trying to make students look dumb." Students reported that he was always willing to see them during office hours, but when they went to his office, he often stood at the door to talk with them, as if to say, "OK, get on with it, then get out." Or he wore dark glasses, sat with his arms folded across his chest, or tapped his fingers on the desk while they asked questions, which he would answer with short sentences.

Extreme cases? Perhaps. But every description in this account comes from a real Professor Wolf. For each of these people, the relationship of students to professor is a subservient one. Students are expected to do what they are told. Professors wield a big stick in the form of the grade and credit in the class. The class becomes an opportunity to exercise that power or to display brilliance—sometimes at the expense of the students—or both.

In contrast, the best teachers we studied displayed not power but an investment in the students. Their practices stem from a concern with learning that is strongly felt and powerfully communicated. "Most important," Jeanette Norden argues, "our teaching must communicate that we have an investment in the students and that we do what we do because we care about our students as people and as learners." Yes, there are rules, and sometimes strongly stated ones (Norden, for example, insists that if students take her class they agree to attend all "personal days"), but those requirements are pared to the bone and stem from a contract—no, a strong bond of trust—between the teacher and the learner. In that relationship, the teacher has effectively said, as one of the study subjects put it, "I will do everything possible to help you learn and develop your abilities, but you must decide if you want to engage in this experience. If you do decide to join this enterprise, there are some things you must resolve to do to make it worthwhile for you and others in the group."

Outstanding teachers recognize that those rules do not constitute intellectual or artistic standards. Thus rules can be changed to fit individual needs whereas the standards of achievement cannot. Consider, for example, the story that began this chapter. To the math professor, there were two primary considerations in dealing with all students, including the young man with test anxiety. He wanted to help them learn calculus, and he wanted to know whether they were doing so. That sounds like a reasonable and normal set of concerns, but it is not what many other professors would regard as most important. When we presented this story and others like it to a variety of different professors who were not in the study, it became clear that many of them wanted their students to perform well on calculus examinations, which is not necessarily the same as learning calculus. But because performance *on the examination* became the goal of the education—rather than learning calculus—they insisted that every student jump through exactly the same hoops. In their view, justice demanded little consideration of the individual needs of each student. The process became a game with rules for adding up scores and marking winners and losers rather than an attempt to help each student achieve his or her best and to assess the outcomes accurately.

With the rejection of power came an equally important and powerful trust. "The most important aspect of my teaching," one instructor told us in a theme we heard frequently, "is the relationship of trust that develops between me and my students." That trust meant that the teachers believed students wanted to learn, and they assumed, until proven otherwise, that they could learn. That attitude found reflection in scores of small and large practices. It led to high expectations and to the habit of looking inward for any problems rather than blaming some alleged student deficiency. "I want to make my class user friendly," a management school professor told us, "because I'm interested in students getting it. If they don't learn, I fail as a professor."

Trust also produced little if any worry on the part of teachers that students might try to trick them. While some professors seemed limited in their choice of pedagogical tools by some worry that a student might be able to cheat the system, the highly effective threw caution to the wind and did what they thought would benefit learning. They might use take-home examinations, for example, while many of their colleagues were reluctant to do so, frozen by the thought that some people might not do their own work. Most important, the successful teachers we studied exhibited trust because it was such an integral part of their attitudes and conceptions, and the way they thought about their students radiated through every encounter they had with them. Such trust was evident regardless of the nature of the students or the institution. We saw it among highly effective teachers at open admissions colleges and at the most selective places. In contrast, we encountered less effective teachers everywhere who were convinced that the gods of academia had stuffed their classes with nothing but lazy anti-intellectuals.

Professors who established a special trust with their students often displayed a kind of openness in which they might, from time to time, talk about their intellectual journey, its ambitions, triumphs, frustrations, and failures, and encourage students to be similarly reflective and candid. Many of our subjects occasionally told stories about what drew them into their fields, about the questions that swelled in their minds and how those inquiries led to other interests that eventually animated their intellectual life. They shared with students their secrets about learning, how they remembered something, or the analogies they made in their mind as they built their own understanding. Such public confessions never became a parade of old war stories—that could become deadly—rather, they emerged discreetly and judiciously, setting a tone for similar discussions among the students. "When I heard my professor tell me how much difficulty she first had with chemistry," a young woman from Pennsylvania told us, "that gave me the confidence I needed to learn it. I used to think these people were just born with all this knowledge. That's the way a lot of them act."

"The trouble with most of us," Craig Nelson is fond of saying, "is that we teach like we were god. There is no sense of the contingency of our knowledge."

That trust and openness produced an interactive atmosphere in which students could ask questions without reproach or embarrassment, and in which a variety of views and ways to understand could be freely discussed. "There's no such thing as a stupid question in my class," a sociologist told us. On the first day of class, he reminds students that others will appreciate the questions they ask. "I try to make students feel relaxed and challenged, but always comfortable enough to challenge me and each other," one teacher emphasized. "My students learn from each other," another noted. "No one is an expert in everything, so they can learn from the collective insights that the students bring to the classroom."

"Everybody can contribute and each contribution is unique," Paul Baker emphasized. "I want each of my students to understand that no one else in the world will bring his or her particular set of experiences and body chemistry to the class. Everybody has something special to offer, an original perspective."[1]

With that trust and openness came an unabashed and frequently expressed sense of awe and curiosity about life, and that too affected the relationships that emerged. It appeared most frequently and prominently in people who had a sense of humility about themselves and their own learning. They might realize what they knew and even that their own knowledge was far greater than that of their students, but they also understood how much they didn't know and that in the great scheme of things their own accomplishments placed them relatively close to those of their students. David Besanko, who teaches in the Kellogg School of Management at Northwestern, often attributed his own success as a teacher to "how slow I am." He told students and colleagues alike that he often struggled to comprehend many of the important concepts he used in his discipline, and that struggle allowed him to understand more fully the difficulties others might have with those ideas.

A similar humility marked others in the study. They saw themselves as students of life, fellow travelers in search of some small glimpse of "the truth." They talked frequently about a journey they took *with* their students in search of a better understanding, or told us stories about insights that students had developed that influenced their own comprehension. While many of their colleagues might disdain the struggles of their students ("I don't suffer fools lightly," a former dean and university president loved to say), the best teachers generally felt a bond between themselves and their students in humankind's struggles to know anything. They even found power in their ignorance. "You have to be confused," Dudley Herschbach, the Nobel Prize-winning chemist from Harvard, confessed, "before you can reach a new level of understanding anything."

In many disciplines, especially within the sciences, some practitioners act as if they are, as Jerry Farber put it long ago, "high priest(s) of arcane mysteries," playing out an ego game in which they pretend to have special powers most students can only envy. They seem to cultivate in their students what one of our subjects called "a befuddlement degradation," the sense that only "smart men can possibly comprehend this material and that if you can't understand what I'm saying, that must mean I'm a lot smarter than you are." This attitude is probably what led so many students we interviewed to say that their "worst" teachers acted superior to their students but could not communicate clearly. As one person put it, "She is so far above me, so brilliant, but she can't bring it down to our level." For these professors, their discipline is, as Farber put it, "an arena for expertise, a ledger book for the ego."[2]

Contrast such attitudes and behaviors with the way Herschbach talked about his discipline (in a manner so typical of people in the study). In so many introductory science classes, the chemist observed, students encounter what they see as "a frozen body of dogma" that must be memorized and regurgitated. Yet in the "real science you're not too worried about the right answer . . . Real science recognizes that you have an advantage over practically any other human enterprise because what you are after—call it truth or understanding—waits patiently for you while you screw up." He spoke about the humbling experience of standing before nature and trying again and again to figure it out. "Nature," he said, "speaks in many tongues and they are all alien. What a scientist is trying to do is to decipher one of those dialects." If scientists make progress, he concluded, they do so "because nature doesn't change and we just keep trying. It's not because we are particularly smart but because we are stubborn."

Herschbach's approach illustrates well the intersection between the way the best professors conceived of themselves and their discipline and how they treated students. He and others were no longer high priests, selfishly guarding the doors to the kingdom of knowledge to make themselves look more important. They were fellow students—no, fellow human beings—struggling with the mysteries of the universe, human society, historical development, or whatever. They found affinity with their students in their own ignorance and curiosity, in their love of life and beauty, in their mixture of respect and fear, and in that mix they discovered more similarities than differences between themselves and the people who populated their classes. A sense of awe at the world and the human condition stood at the center of their relationships with those students.

Most important, that humility, that fear, that veneration of the unknown spawned a kind of quiet conviction on the part of the best teachers that they and their students could do great things together. They had a vigorous respect both for the limits of their own achievements and for the monumental feats that any human being racks up in learning to navigate life. They believed that their own intellectual achievements stemmed primarily from perseverance rather than from any special talent, but they also marveled at all human accomplishments—including those of their students. That mixture of humility and pride, fear and determination was most apparent in the way they approached their own failures as teachers.

"When my teaching fails," John Lachs, a philosophy professor at Vanderbilt, told us, "it is because of something I have failed to do." For Lachs and others, even the recognition and definition of shortcomings distinguished their thinking. Many professors never saw any problems with their own teaching, or they believed they could do little to correct deficiencies because "great teachers are born, not made." In contrast, the most effective instructors did see problems if they failed to reach a student, but they tried to keep any lack of success from affecting their confidence that they could fix the problem with more effort.

Sure, they became frustrated with students at times and occasionally displayed impatience, but because they were willing to face the failures of teaching and believed in their capacity to solve problems, they tried not to become defensive with their students or build a wall around themselves. Instead, they tried to take their students seriously as human beings and treated them the way they might treat any colleague, with fairness, compassion, and concern. That approach found reflection in what they taught, how they taught it, and how they evaluated students, but it also appeared in attempts to understand their students' lives, cultures, and aspirations. It even emerged in their willingness to see their students outside of class.

Derrick Bell began teaching law at Harvard in the 1960s. By the early 1970s, he had become the first African American to win tenure in the law school there. In 1980, he left Harvard to become a dean at the University of Oregon, but returned to Massachusetts five years later because he felt his colleagues on the West Coast had failed to give an Asian American woman proper consideration for a faculty position. In 1992 he left his tenured post at Harvard, this time in protest over the lack of sufficient progress in bringing women of color to the faculty. He came to New York University as a visiting professor that year and simply stayed, serving on a series of one-year appointments.

Over the years, Bell toyed with his course in constitutional law, building the learning experience around a series of hypothetical cases that raised important constitutional issues. He wrote each case as a small but compelling story, filled with characters whose lives became entangled with the way we understand the Constitution. Bell knew how to use words to paint a picture and raise an issue, a craft he had refined in a series of allegorical stories published in the 1980s and 1990s, including one that was turned into an HBO film in 1994. His fictional heroine, Geneva Crenshaw, populated those stories, but in the constitutional "hypos" he wrote about ordinary people who became caught up in issues of equal protection and family rights. In time, he invited his students to write similar stories, and their work contributed to a growing body of hypos that he used in the course. In each life, they embedded important constitutional questions.

Students who take the class read an enormous body of material, but the "hypos" form the backbone of the learning environment, luring students into serious consideration of matters of liberty, justice, compassion, fairness, and due process. The stories raise the issues in compelling ways, pulling at both the intellect and the emotions of the students. The students learn by doing, by participating in judicial deliberations, by writing, by exchanging ideas, by arguing a case, by making decisions, and by getting feedback on their efforts. "The structure and expectations for this 'participatory learning' course," Bell says in the first sentence they read about the course, "differ substantially from the norm." Everybody reads everything, but each student works with two or three others to argue a particular case before the entire class, which acts as a giant court, questioning, debating, and ultimately voting on the hypothetical outcome. Everything Bell wants them to learn to do intellectually he embeds in the process. Nothing is extraneous to their learning.

In his choice of language, Bell gives his students a strong sense of control. Everything he asks them to do has a justification and explanation, all tied to their learning. When he asks them to pick a hypothetical case at the beginning of the semester, he reminds them that such a process will encourage them to review the entire course as they begin their studies. When he talks about the "op-ed" pieces they will write, he says that "students will have the *opportunity* [emphasis added]" to post eight to ten such articles "unless they feel strongly motivated" to post more. Rather than stressing the minimum requirement, he emphasizes that they should post "no more" than twelve, but they can post additional comments in another section of the Web pages.

He invites them into a community of learners in which they will contribute to the exchange of ideas and to each other's education, sometimes reminding them of the obligations they have as citizens of that body. "These reflections," he says of the op-ed pieces, "are an important part of the course learning process. They should be posted in time for possible discussion" in the next class. "Late papers," he emphasizes, "will harm" other students. "Posting on the Web page," he reminds the students, "makes your views available to everyone." As for quality, the students should ask themselves, "Is this a piece I would not mind having published in a daily paper?"

In the early years of the course, he asked students to turn in hard copies of their reflections, but the advent of the Internet allowed him to create exchanges between students. They now submit their work online and then respond to one another. "Here is the real heart of the class, with students literally speaking to one another and getting responses," Bell says. "I am not in it at all." In class, students lead an hour-long discussion of these postings while Bell listens and occasionally comments or asks questions. The exchanges in cyberspace and in class, he argues, raise "the level of understanding."

Bell conveys a strong investment in the lives, careers, and development of his students. That commitment appears in everything he does for them. It shines in the extensive Web resources that he assembles for their use, in the notes he provides, in the hypothetical cases he so carefully crafts, in the arrangements he makes for students to support one another, in the feedback he gives them, and in the environment he shapes. He arranges for a small group of outstanding students from the previous year to help those currently enrolled write their briefs and bench memos. He provides students with feedback on their efforts, and arranges for more advanced students to do the same. The final grade includes an extensive written memorandum on their work. "The students are so impressive," he told us. "My challenge is structuring courses that give them a chance to teach one another, both the course material and their life perspectives."

That investment in his students is also apparent in Bell's attention to improving the course and in the joy he takes in doing so. Even after nearly forty years of teaching, he still regularly calls the teaching center to ask for suggestions and comments on his work. "I am the Walter Alston professor of law," Bells jokes in a reference to the manager of the Brooklyn Dodgers who served for twenty years on a series of one-year contracts, "but I'm determined to equal Alston's record. "I will be 81 then, but if my health holds up, I hope to make it . . . they will have to pour me out of this job."

Finally, that investment is apparent in the way he treats his students with courtesy and dignity. Much of the class time belongs to the students, but he takes a few minutes at the beginning of each session to talk with them about their lives and to share personal moments from his own. On occasion, he talks briefly about his family, and in those references he blurs the distinctions between private and professional lives. He listens to students, even when they strongly disagree with his views, and more likely than not he asks them a question rather than tells them they are wrong.

At the end of class, Bell gathers the team responsible for the day's case and takes group pictures, posing the students this way and that with all of the concern, love, and pride of a parent at a graduation ceremony. When the pictures are done, he takes the team members to a little Italian restaurant in Greenwich Village. Over dinner, he talks extensively with each student, explores their lives and ambitions, marvels at their accomplishments, shares their concerns, and engages in an ongoing conversation about the issues that animate the class.

"I took a walk with my wife one Sunday morning in the Village," a student told us at one of those dinners, "and we came across the NYU law school. I said to my wife, 'Derrick Bell teaches here. I would love to study with him.' 'Why don't you apply,' she urged me. So I did and here I am. It is a dream come true. He has such a sharp mind, but he is also so decent to his students. He treats them with respect and concern."

When I neared the end of my first semester of teaching more than thirty years ago, I began to prepare the final examination. In the days before giving the test, I talked with several colleagues about the kinds of questions I might ask. We met over lunch or coffee and toyed with this item and that one, building clever little puzzles that intrigued us and promised to confound the students. Our efforts paid rich dividends, stumping most of the people who took the exam. I had set high standards and put my students through their paces, or at least so I thought at the time.

That examination, however, like many others I have encountered since then, said little about the intellectual or personal achievements of my students. It did not even tell me much, if anything, about my teaching. Most regrettable, it encouraged strategic learning rather than deep thinking. It emphasized reproduction of what I had told the class rather than the ability to reason with concepts and information, and it encouraged students merely to focus on guessing which questions I might ask.

Like so many teachers, I failed to understand that testing and grading are not incidental acts that come at the end of teaching but powerful aspects of education that have an enormous influence on the entire enterprise of helping and encouraging students to learn. Without an adequate assessment, neither teachers nor students can comprehend the progress the learners are making, and instructors can little understand whether their efforts are best suited to their students and objectives. A teacher can even quite inadvertently undermine all else that might be done to create the best learning environments, often fostering strategic learning.

Unfortunately, many of the traditional practices in testing and grading and even the emerging methods of evaluating teaching do little better than I did then, and often without any appreciation for the shortfalls. Much of the conventional wisdom on grading students—what we can call assessment—often seems trapped in a morass of secondary considerations that have little to do with learning. Many examinations may capture the students' ability to take certain kinds of tests but reflect little about the way students think (remember the physics students who could ace the final examination yet still think about motion in pre-Newtonian terms). Meanwhile, discussions of how to appraise teaching—what we can call evaluation—largely center around the merits and demerits of student rating forms. At best, they concentrate on whether teachers use acceptable methods of instruction. At worst, they produce much hand-ringing and the surrendered pronouncement that evaluation of teaching can't be done.

In contrast, we found professors who have broken with tradition to forge fundamentally different approaches to both assessment and evaluation, and in those differences to answer questions that have long plagued conversations about such matters. Not surprisingly, these are the same people I've talked about throughout this book. In their hands, evaluation and assessment become intertwined, supporting each other in ways that deliberately benefit learning. When they assess their students, they do so in part to test their own efforts to facilitate learning. When they evaluate their teaching, they do so by looking at learning, both the objectives and the outcomes.

ASSESSING STUDENTS

The outstanding teachers used assessment to help students learn, not just to rate and rank their efforts. Dudley Herschbach told us, "I want to help them learn something about themselves so they can become better learners and thinkers. I'm not interested in just adding up so many scores like a cash register." Examinations and assignments become a way to help students understand their progress in learning, and they also help evaluate teaching. "I use each examination," Jeanette Norden explains, "to tell me how well I helped my students learn. If I see a pattern of misunderstanding, I will have to do something to 're-teach' the material."

Many traditional teachers with whom we spoke clearly thought about grades as a way, as one professor put it, "to separate the sheep from the goats." The notion that the "goats" might reflect something about the teacher's abilities apparently didn't occur to them, and didn't even make sense in their ideas about teaching, learning, assessment, and evaluation. In those conceptions, schooling is primarily a way to certify, to pick the best and brightest rather than to help all students learn better. "I think," one teacher told us, "that many of my colleagues think that their chief responsibility is to find ability rather than to encourage its development."

Equally important, evaluation and assessment stress learning rather than performance. To understand this learning-based approach, let's contrast it with the more traditional, performance-based thinking. In that conventional model, students' grades come primarily from their ability to comply with the dictates of the course. In the best of circumstances, those demands may have originated with some reasonable learning considerations, but the origins are sometimes forgotten as the requirements take on a life of their own. In the worst cases, the requirements stem from what appears to be the convenience of the professor rather than from the legitimate learning goals of the students. In all cases, a grade emerges from how well students perform the required tasks within the dictates of the course.

In a learning-centered approach, however, the questions change. Rather than asking if the student said anything in class or did a certain assignment and made a certain score, the professor asks what we will call the fundamental assessment question: What kind of intellectual and personal development do I want my students to enjoy in this class, and what evidence might I collect about the nature and progress of their development?

Note several points about this question. First, it assumes that learning is a developmental process rather than only a question of acquisition. Learning entails primarily intellectual and personal changes that people undergo as they develop new understandings and reasoning abilities. Second, grading becomes not a means to rank but a way to communicate with students. Evidence about learning might come from an examination, a paper, a project, or a conversation, but it is that learning, rather than a score, that professors try to characterize and communicate.

The widely used practice of counting off for late papers offers some illustration of the performance-based approach. It's easy to see that such a policy might have emerged because some instructors thought students should learn to meet a deadline. In other cases, it may have arisen in cases where students depended on each other's work in a community of learners. Yet it persists in disciplines in which scholars do not always face a deadline for their own work, and in classes in which students do not read one another's papers. It is often scored in rigorous and precise fashion, as if such numbers can really capture the degree to which students have internalized a sense of timeliness. The numbers themselves often suggest that the ability to be timely counts as much as—or sometimes even more than—the capacity to do the discipline. Most professors who have such policies don't claim that the ability to meet a deadline is a learning objective or try to create the kind of community of learners that Derrick Bell did (see Chapter 6). They simply count off because they don't like late papers. In their instructions they usually emphasize the penalty rather than, say, the obligations to classmates who are waiting to read the paper. Even those who cite such a policy as a learning objective can seldom if ever point to any evidence that it actually encourages students to be timely or that such habits are likely to stick beyond the confines of the classroom. Thus in many classes the late-paper policy no longer has any learning base, only a performance one.

Consider, for example, what a professor who was not part of the study once wrote on a student's paper: "This is an interesting narrative, but it could be polished. It would help your *grade* [emphasis added] enormously if you would get your papers in on time. Although your paper was four days late, I am cutting the penalty in half." Below the comment, he scribbled "B = 84 minus 20 late penalty. 64 = D." In that note, the professor had provided no reference to learning, only an indication that he had generously cut the student some slack in the points game. The penalty left a chilling reminder that the accumulation of points toward a grade remained the primary objective, even more important, apparently, than the ill-defined notion of "polishing" the paper.

Or consider the literature class in which each student chose a nineteenth-century Russian novel to read, analyze, and report on to the rest of the class. While many students selected short works, one picked Tolstoy's *War and Peace.* As luck would have it, that student drew an early slot to make her report, but given the length and complexity of the book she could not finish in time. Even when she talked to the professor about swapping with a willing classmate, he refused to compromise. The rules of the class exacted a heavy penalty for her ambitious reading plans.

Compare that approach with the practices and thinking of many of the best teachers: They do hope that their students will learn to do the work in a timely manner, but they do not assume that their power over grades can facilitate that learning, or even that a late paper indicates that the student has procrastinated ("there might be all sorts of reasons why the paper is late besides procrastination," one teacher reminded us. "They might be late because they decided to pursue some higher goal for the project or do more work on it."). They believe that extrinsic threats might even be counterproductive.

Instead of threatening, some of these outstanding instructors might try to help their students get organized. One teacher distributes a sheet of paper marked with seven columns and twenty-four rows, a box for every hour in the week. "Mark each hour you will be in class, commuting, sleeping, relaxing, and eating. Now, can you find time to do your homework? You'll need two hours for every hour you are in class. If not, you may not have time to take this class." On the first day of class, many teachers explain the kind of thinking expected for each letter grade and give students a list of dates when various projects should be finished. "If you finish each task by the appointed day," one teacher told his class, "you will make orderly progress toward the goals of the course." He then explained that if they didn't meet the deadline, he simply wouldn't be able to provide them with helpful comments before they did the next assignment. "If you need someone to threaten you if you don't make good progress," one person told students, "then I'm prepared to do that, but take control of your own life." With such approaches, few students submit late work.

In scores of examples, we found an emphasis on learning rather than on performance. Not all teachers followed the same practices, but they often broke with convention, stripping away the layers of tradition that had turned education into an obstacle course. Grades represented an assessment of students' thinking, not whether they met some arbitrary rule. "The quality of the work doesn't change because it is late," one professor explained. "Was the painting on the ceiling of the Sistine Chapel any less beautiful because it ran behind schedule?" That approach also meant that students couldn't rack up points for simply playing the game. While many of the teachers we studied provided students with multiple ways to demonstrate their thinking, they avoided what one person called "arbitrary extra credit," points given to students for doing something that reflected little if anything about their learning (filling out the online ratings of the class, for example).

The performance-based approach is evident in the way professors often try to cultivate and reward class participation. One common approach is to give points every time students open their mouths. When we asked professors outside the study why they offered such incentives, they clearly believed that grades were necessary motivators. Others had identified the capacity to engage in an intellectual exchange as one of the learning objectives of the class and saw the grade for participation as their assessment of how students were shaping up.

Only the last group came close to raising the fundamental assessment question so dear to our subjects. The others had established rules for behavior within the class and marked students according to how well they met those rules. Yet even that last group emphasized scores rather than assessments of student learning and development. These professors made judgments and assigned numbers, but they didn't offer constructive feedback. With striking ease they decided that they could assign a number to represent the capacity that students had developed to participate in an intellectual exchange. They might quibble over what that number might be and how much it might count, but they never shrank from the task of devising that value and assigning a letter to someone's thoughts. Indeed, most of them argued that reducing their judgment to a number made it all the more precise, almost "scientific," and certainly "objective." Missing was any sense of intellectual definition, of critique, of saying to students, here is what makes your contributions valuable, here is how you have developed, and here are ways in which you can continue to mature. Here is what I mean by a "polished" paper.

In contrast, the learning-based approach so common to our subjects tried to build a course that enticed students into the serious consideration of important questions. Students' conversations might help indicate how they were approaching the problems, but the professors would never rely on that evidence alone to make final assessments. The class discussions could give students a chance to practice conversing and receive substantive constructive criticism, but they didn't become a scoring match based on how many times a student spoke.

PRACTICES

To make learning-based assessment work, the best teachers try to find out as much as possible about their students, "not so I can make judgments about them," one instructor explained, "but so that I can help them learn." He and others began early in the term to collect information about their students. They explored their ambitions, their approaches to and conceptions of learning, the ways they reasoned, the mental models they brought with them, their temperaments, their habits of the heart and mind, and the daily matters that occupied their attention. Paul Baker wanted to know "which of the five senses each student identified with the most." In his Integration of Abilities class he helped students explore sight, sound, smell, taste, and kinesthetic movement. Through a series of exercises he began early in the term, he helped each student "find out what a person's real talent is." He explained that some people, for example, "don't realize that line and color are really what speak to them. So you help the person find which of his senses is the strongest. Some people may be strong in a whole lot of them, but there's always one or two predominant senses. Then you teach to that."[1]

Some outstanding teachers use survey forms or what might be called in the broadest sense a pre-test. On the first day of class, other people give students a list of the five to ten major questions the course will help them answer. They then ask the class members to rank their interests in each question. Still others make a habit of talking with students both before and after class to gather such information more casually and informally. A few professors in the study regularly go to lunch with students. They might establish a routine schedule of eating with small groups of students until everyone in the class has had a chance to attend. Ralph Lynn spent the first day of each class giving students a kind of vocabulary test that told him a great deal about their thinking and understanding. While he dictated the words for students to define, he interspersed that exercise with his own efforts to call each student by name, all with much good humor as he went up and down the rows testing his own memory of names and faces while he gathered insights into students' thinking.

The particular exercise mattered far less than did the attempt to understand students in all their complexity as they came into the classroom. Experience counted heavily. Seasoned professors developed strong and often detailed impressions of their students, understandings that they had built over time. That is not to say, however, that conceptions became frozen artifacts, old yellowed notes in the teacher's mind that changed little over the years. Rather, we found even among people who had taught for several decades a kind of fresh, "what-are-they-going-to-be-like-this-term" sense of inquiry as they approached each new class. They might have strong hypotheses that had emerged from years of experience, but each individual they encountered required a new testing of old theories. Most important, the best teachers seemed to gather that information not to judge but to help.

The process of getting to know students continued throughout the term, with an emphasis on how students changed or stayed the same as a result of the class and how they reacted to the course. Again, a variety of techniques seemed to work equally well. Some people asked students to write immediate responses to a particular class, taking two or three minutes at the end to explain what major conclusions they had drawn, why they had drawn those conclusions, and what major questions remained in their minds. Others regularly gave students small exercises that could reflect their thinking. In large classes, some teachers created permanent small groups and then met regularly with representatives from each one.

Many professors use some form of anonymous feedback after three or four weeks of class. One such procedure, called a small group analysis, utilizes the resources of a teaching center or a colleague. Someone goes into the class while the instructor leaves the room. The consultant divides the students into small groups or pairs and asks each team to spend six or seven minutes discussing three questions: In what ways has the instruction/instructor helped you learn in this course? Can you suggest some changes in the instruction/course that would better help you learn? If the course/instruction has helped you learn, what is the nature of that learning? Each team receives the questions on paper and is encouraged to take notes on their discussions. After six or seven minutes, the consultant brings the groups back together and gets feedback from some of them while inviting others to share any major additions to or disagreements with what they heard from their colleagues. The whole process takes less than twenty minutes and allows the consultant both to clarify (to ask those questions that we have all wanted to pursue when we read students' comments) and to verify (to find out if there are any divisions in the ranks).

USING EXAMINATIONS

Collecting information about students is the first step toward using assessment to help them improve and in crafting a learning rather than a performance base for the process. The second step helps students understand and use the criteria by which they will be judged. That entails spelling out that standard as clearly as possible. When we talked with some teachers outside the study about this approach, many were simply baffled. Because they think of learning as remembering and testing as recalling, they could not imagine how anyone might be able to judge their own work, except perhaps to look up right answers. If they tried to define the standards of their courses, they often talked about how many points each assignment counted and what it took to make an A.

In contrast, the teachers in the study talked extensively about the learning students must achieve to earn each possible letter grade. What kind of abstract reasoning abilities must students develop? What must they come to understand? How must they apply that understanding? To what kinds of problems? What must they be able to analyze, synthesize, and evaluate? What are the criteria by which they will make those evaluations? Into what kinds of conversations should they be able to engage? With whom?

In this conception of assessment, the primary goal is to help students learn to think about their own thinking so they can use the standards of the discipline or profession to recognize shortcomings and correct their reasoning as they go. It isn't to rank students. Grading on a curve, therefore, makes no sense in this world. Students must meet certain standards of excellence, and while none of those standards may be absolute, they are not arbitrary either. Grades represent clearly articulated levels of achievement. "If all of the students make an A," more than one person told us, "they get an A. If they all make F's, that's what they get."

Nor does it make sense in this world to use the examination as a game in which students spend their preparation time trying to predict what the teacher might ask. "I want my students to prepare themselves intellectually, to concentrate on what they understand and how they reason with what they comprehend," Paul Travis told us. "I don't want them to spend time trying to outguess me about what fact I might ask them to recall. If they understand, they know which information is worth remembering." For Travis, that means he gives mostly take-home examinations. "I don't want to test only for recall or recognition but for how well they understand." For others, it means that they lay out the major questions of the final examination on the first day of class. In math and other problem-oriented disciplines, it means helping students understand concepts that will allow them to solve the problems rather than merely emphasizing the mechanical practice of problem-solving. Rather than performing calculus in front of students week after week and merely asking them to repeat the process in daily homework, Don Saari helps students learn to invent calculus.

Many outstanding teachers give comprehensive examinations with each test replacing the previous one. The first test covers material from the beginning of the course, but so do all subsequent examinations. "Meningitis," Norden tells her students, "is just as important at the end of the course as it is at the beginning." The final deals with the entire course. "You don't just learn something just to kiss it goodbye once the examination is over," Ralph Lynn said frequently. In such a system, students can try, come up short, receive feedback on their efforts, and try again on a subsequent examination. What they understand and can do intellectually by the end of the course matters more than anything else.

While some people worry that this system will encourage students to delay studying until the end, the best professors don't let that concern them because they don't use grades to motivate students. They create captivating classes that engage students and win their attention. In fact, many of our subjects told us that they seldom discuss a "grading system" with students, telling them instead about the kinds of comprehension and reasoning abilities expected. They saw no reason to tell students at the beginning of the term that the comprehensive final could count for everything. If students miss a test, they presumably have unforeseen and uncontrollable emergencies. After they miss, one person told us, "you can simply say, 'don't worry. You will have a chance on the next examination because it will cover everything this one did and then some.'"

By making each examination cumulative, professors convey to the students that learning is supposed to be permanent and not just something done to get through a single examination. At the same time, they encourage all students (even those who fail the first or second examination) to keep learning, right up to the final. Furthermore, with such a system, they can use examinations that require sophisticated reasoning skills that stretch the students' abilities and encourage them to improve, making each test more sophisticated than the last one.

When I share these approaches with colleagues in workshops, they sometimes see them as "teaching to the test," a practice that in their minds deserves the most pious scorn. They recognize that tests often do not gather adequate information about the intellectual and personal progress students are making, that they are merely games to be won or lost. Thus preparing students to play those games seems like a loathsome departure from higher intellectual pursuits. In contrast, the best teachers see examinations as extensions of the kind of work that is already taking place in the course. Teachers prepare students to do certain kinds of intellectual work, not to be good test-takers. The examinations ask students to do that work. The goal is to establish congruity between the intellectual objectives of the course and those that the examination assesses.

The learning objectives shape the nature of both instruction and assessment. If the goal is for students to analyze and evaluate arguments and then synthesize the information and ideas into work of their own, the instruction provides them with practice and feedback in doing precisely that, whereas a test or paper might later determine whether they can. If the goal is to develop sufficient understanding to solve problems or learn to think critically, the grade doesn't hinge on how well they can recall information or recognize the correct answer within a limited time.

Most important, the teachers in our study tended to have a strong sense of humility when it came to grades. "I am not infallible," one professor told us in a sentiment we encountered repeatedly, "and I recognize the enormous difficulty of understanding someone's intellectual growth, but my students and I must try to do that. In fact, that's part of my educational mission: to help students try to understand their own learning. In the end, I simply make the best judgment I can." That humility spilled into both their conception of assessment as a carefully reasoned judgment and the limits they placed on the meaning of grades. "I'm not judging anyone," one professor told us, "I'm merely trying to understand something about learning so I can help students continue to learn."

In that spirit, some of the best professors ask students to assess themselves. One frequently used model requests that they provide evidence and conclusion about the nature of their learning. At the end of the semester, they write an argument of 750 to 1,500 words demonstrating how well they can measure their reasoning in process and recognize where it is strong and where it needs improvement.

EVALUATION OF TEACHING

There is a pattern here: every act centers around and ultimately springs from a concern for student learning. That same pattern is readily apparent in the way these teachers think about how to measure their own efforts; it is even reflected in the commitment to do so. To understand what that commitment involves, let's look first at traditional approaches to evaluating teaching.

When we asked conventional teachers about evaluating teaching, they often denied that it could be done, suggesting that in their minds teaching has no standards against which it can be measured. If we pressed them to tell us what kind of questions they might want to answer about someone's teaching, they usually stressed inquiries about methods. That performance-based model judges instructors on whether and how often they conform to certain accepted habits in the classroom. Do they use the latest technology, generate class discussions, call on students by name, write clearly on the board, return examinations promptly, limit lectures, use discussions or case studies, and lecture clearly?

No doubt, these questions point to good practices, but they still focus on what the professor does rather than on what the students learn. A professor could get high marks on all the conventionally right practices yet have little positive influence on student learning. In contrast, our subjects take a learning-based approach, asking the fundamental evaluation question, Does the teaching help and encourage students to learn in ways that make a sustained, substantial and positive difference in the way they think, act, or feel—without doing them any major harm?

That question breaks into four subquestions, all prominent in the thinking of the teachers we studied, regardless of their discipline: (1) Is the material worth learning (and, perhaps, appropriate to the curriculum)? (2) Are my students learning what the course is supposedly teaching? (3) Am I helping and encouraging the students to learn (or do they learn despite me)? (4) Have I harmed my students (perhaps fostering short-term learning with intimidation tactics, discouraging rather than stimulating additional interest in the field, fostering strategic or bulimic rather than deep learning, neglecting the needs of a diverse student population, or failing to evaluate students' learning accurately)?

To answer these questions, the best teachers engage in an extensive examination of their learning objectives, reviewing students' work as a reflection of their learning, analyzing the kinds of standards and methods used in assessing that work, and looking closely at the levels of learning expected. To assess their learning objectives, they follow important intellectual developments emerging within and outside their disciplines. They might even seek review of those objectives from a colleague, but they also frequently contribute to the public discussion about educational goals, pushing the boundaries of acceptable learning within the courses they teach. When Jeanette Norden first introduced the goal of personal as well as intellectual development for her medical students, not all her colleagues were pleased. Today, such ambitions have become accepted practice in medical education.

STUDENT RATINGS

In the first chapter, I mentioned that if you ask students the right questions, their answers can help you evaluate the quality of teaching. We reached that conclusion after looking both at the research on and our subjects' use of student ratings. From that research we know, for example, that if you ask students something like, "Rate your learning in this course," their responses usually have a high positive correlation with independent measures of their learning. Behind that finding, however, there has always lurked the possibility that students might not have acceptable notions of what counts as good learning. What would happen, for example, if students expected simply to memorize a lot of facts while the professor wanted them to analyze, synthesize, and evaluate? Would they give their teacher low scores, and if they did, what value would such ratings have? Conversely, couldn't they theoretically give superior marks to instructors who demanded only recall? Noel Entwistle and Hilary Tait, two Scottish researchers, became interested in those questions and found that different kinds of learners might give the same experience conflicting ratings. Deep learners said they liked courses that pushed them to explore conceptual meanings and implications, whereas their classmates who were surface learners hated such experiences. Students who thought learning meant memorization praised courses that valued recall while those who expected to reason on a higher level reported that they didn't learn much.

Some teachers believe that those findings discredit student ratings, but in general our subjects saw it differently. One professor put it this way, "If my students are satisfied with learning trivia and they tell the world I do a good job helping them learn, that's a compliment I'd just as soon forgo." Yet he and others could not dismiss the opposite results. "I have some students," he reported, "who come into my class thinking that all they have to do is memorize and regurgitate. The class frustrates them at first because I'm asking them to understand and reason. In the end, if they give me low marks, it's because I've failed to affect their concepts of what it means to learn my discipline." The ratings point to a real weakness in the course—the failure to reach students educationally and help them understand the nature of the learning expected of them—not just to the capricious nature of students' opinions.

As another teacher put it, "High ratings from students indicate success only if I am satisfied with the quality of what I'm asking them to do intellectually, and that is reflected not in the ratings but in my syllabus, assignments, and the ways I grade their work. Low ratings, on the other hand, usually tell me I've failed to reach my students."

Other kinds of questions also mattered to these teachers. "If I want to know whether I've challenged my students intellectually or stimulated their interest," one professor told us, "what better way than to ask them."[2] What mattered most, however, was not the class averages but what percentage of the class these teachers reached "educationally." Did they score an average of 3.8 on a 6-point scale because most of the responses clustered in the middle, or because most students gave them high marks while a few others put them at the bottom? Why didn't they reach those disgruntled students? How could they improve their efforts? Could they be satisfied with reaching most students while displeasing others?

TOWARD A SYSTEM OF EVALUATING TEACHING

As we listened to these ideas and questions, we began to wonder if we could use them to fashion a better summative evaluation of teaching. After all, if we are to learn from the insights of highly effective teachers, we must make good judgments about what constitutes effective teaching. In the end, we felt that one of the most important lessons of this study is that teaching must be judged using a learning perspective. Individual instructors must make informed and wise decisions about the quality of their own efforts if they expect to improve them. Institutions must rate the quality of teaching, both so they can help people improve and ultimately so they can keep the best teachers.

In recent years, many faculty members have put together "teaching portfolios." For most, that gruesome process means they throw everything imaginable about teaching into a box and ship it off to the department chair or dean. That container approach reflects little thought about the meaning of good teaching and often produces collections that evaluators find useless. In contrast, others have begun to treat the portfolio as a kind of scholarly argument about the quality of teaching. Like any such argument, it begins with a careful and honest collection of evidence and moves toward using that evidence to draw conclusions about the nature and qualities of the teaching.[3]

That argument attempts to answer fundamental questions. Not every discipline is interested in the same inquiries (historians, for example, usually don't care whether their courses help students pass the national boards in medicine), but all professors should be interested in what I earlier called the fundamental evaluation question and the four subquestions teased out of it.

What will count as good evidence to answer these questions? That depends on the particular question or subquestion you are trying to answer. For some issues, student ratings offer strong evidence; for others, only the syllabus, examples of student work, or the critique of a colleague might do. Any good process should rely on appropriate sources of data, which are then *compiled* and *interpreted* by an evaluator or evaluative committee. Student remarks and ratings, in other words, are not evaluations; they are one set of data that an evaluator can take into consideration. The same can be said for self-evaluations and the results of peer or administrative observations.

The teaching portfolio then becomes a scholarly case—evidence and conclusions that answers questions. For example, such an argument might provide answers to the following questions: What have you tried to help and encourage students to learn? Why are those learning objectives worth achieving for the course you are teaching? What strategies did you use? Were those strategies effective in helping students learn? Why or why not? What did your students learn as a result of your teaching? [If they are not learning what you want them to learn, why not?] Did you stimulate their interest in the subject? Those arguments would require careful and rigorous thought. Rather than simply gathering material—student ratings, syllabus, and so on—and sending it to the evaluator, the faculty member would offer a synthetic and carefully organized case. Thus the burden of establishing connections with the evidence and offering coherence throughout would fall on the teacher—who, in turn, would benefit enormously from the process of self-analysis.

In this scheme, an evaluation is an informed attempt to answer important questions, but it requires difficult decisions and can't be reduced to a formula. Professors and their evaluators should focus on the qualities of learning objectives and the efforts to help students achieve them rather than on numbers. What does the teaching contribute to student learning? Does the instructor expect ambitious and creative learning that makes important contributions to discussions about student learning within the discipline? Do those objectives reflect the highest scientific and scholarly standards? Is there any reason to believe that the instructor helps any of the students to achieve the highest quality of work? What quality of work do most students produce? Has the instructor done any harm?

Peer observations may not be good evidence: professors tend to give high marks to colleagues who teach the way they do and lower ratings to those who do not—regardless of the learning. Furthermore, an observer who sits in on only one or two classes may not get a clear picture of what really goes on.[4] We are interested not in the specific methods the teacher uses but in whether he or she helps and encourages students to learn on an appropriate level. Other observers (students) are in the class on a regular basis to furnish a broader report on how well the class is going.

Peers can, however, provide essential comments on the qualities of the learning objectives. They can look at the syllabus, the way students are assessed, the nature of assignments, reports from the teacher, and even examples of student work to understand the nature of those objectives. They can then use that understanding to make their report. Colleagues can also observe each other to provide strictly formative feedback and start a conversation about teaching.

In short, a teacher should think about teaching (in a single session or an entire course) as a serious intellectual act, a kind of scholarship, a creation; he or she should then develop a case, complete with evidence, exploring the intellectual (and perhaps artistic) meaning and qualities of that teaching. Each case would lay out the argument in an essay. That narrative would explain the qualities of the learning objectives, what the professor has done to foster their achievement, and how the instructor has measured progress. It would also cite the evidence from syllabi, assignment sheets, student ratings, or other sources that support those explanations. "If you want to know what I think is really important to learn," David Besanko told us, "look at what I test." How much of the examination depends on simple recall? How will comprehension reflect itself? Where are students expected to apply, analyze, synthesize, or evaluate? The teacher would then attach in an appendix the evidence cited in the narrative.

To evaluate teaching we then assess the argument. The case becomes the pedagogical equivalent of the scholarly paper, a document intended to capture the scholarship of teaching. While a university consensus might define the general protocols, individual teachers would choose the final form and content of the argument—much as they do now with scholarly papers. This conception of the case allows individual freedom in determining the data of evaluation, but still requires careful and rigorous thought on the part of the teacher.

I have outlined here a procedure that should work well for most faculty members, but departments, schools, and the university must decide who will review these cases. Ultimately, the process depends on how well the evaluators understand human learning. It requires faculties to talk about the nature of learning in the field and begin to craft an epistemological literature in each discipline and course. It demands attention to the science of human learning, to the vast and growing body of research and theoretical literature on how people learn, what it means to learn, and how best to foster it.

To implement this program, departments, schools, and universities would first identify evaluators, help them become familiar with learning and evaluation issues, and begin the discussion about the standards of teaching quality that will be expected. Many disciplines have a long history of discussing what students should be able to do intellectually, physically, or emotionally; others do not, but all departments will have to engage in that conversation. For some, the expectations are well established and fairly exact; for others, they are more general. Some subjects resist any attempt to spell out a list of what students should be taught, and rightfully so, but all disciplines have intellectual or artistic standards that they can apply to this conversation, in much the same way that they have always applied them to questions about the quality of research or artistic products.

That conversation should also go beyond the goals of particular disciplines and address the issues of a broader curriculum. For undergraduate programs—and perhaps for others—that means asking not just about what students should learn in particular

courses but about the kind of personal and intellectual development they should experience as a result of their entire education
and how each course contributes to that process.

Finally, some central points bear repeating for the sake of emphasis and clarity:

1. If we ask students the right question, their answers can help
   evaluators make judgments about the quality of teaching,
   but student ratings are not, by themselves, evaluations.[5]
2. Averages can emerge from a variety of distributions of
   ratings. They may come from all the numbers clustered fairly
   close to the mean. They may come from a combination of
   both high and low ratings. Each distribution might suggest
   something quite different about the success of the teaching.
   In the former case, the instructor might be only marginally
   successful in reaching everyone, while in the latter, the instructor may be highly successful in helping most students
   but fail completely with others. Which kind of teacher does
   the department want? What can help each one improve?
3. Some external factors beyond the control of the instructor
   can influence the way students respond to certain questions.
   An evaluator should take these factors into consideration
   when using the information to make evaluations. Students
   who take courses to satisfy general interest or as a major
   elective tend to give slightly higher ratings; students who
   take courses to satisfy a major or general *requirement* tend
   to give slightly lower ratings. Prior student interest in the
   subject can account for as much as 5.1 percent of a rating.
   Thus senior courses filled with students who report high
   interest before taking a nonrequired course should expect
   slightly higher ratings than introductory-level classes filled
   with students with low prior interest or students who are
   required to take the class.[6]

4. The literature on the correlations between grades and student ratings is long and complex. Student ratings tend to be slightly higher when students expect to receive higher grades, but this does not necessarily mean that grade leniency accounts for the differences. Research has found that students, in general, tend to give higher ratings to courses they regard as intellectually challenging *and* helpful in meeting those challenges, and lower ratings to courses that are easy and in which they do not learn much. Furthermore, students give higher ratings when (1) they are highly motivated and (2) they are learning more and can thus expect to get higher grades.[7]

5. The best way to determine if a course is leniently graded is through a review of course materials and methods and practices of evaluating students. Lenient grading, however, does not necessarily mean less learning. Because of the different standards by which faculty members assign different letter grades, the only way to determine levels of learning is to look in detail at actual student performances (the papers they write, the types of questions they can answer, the problems they can solve, or the performances they give) and the way those performances change over time; mere class grade-point averages cannot provide that information.

With a robust system of evaluation, we can continue to explore what the best teachers do that makes them so effective. We can have rich conversations about our educational objectives and how best to achieve them. We can apply one of the central conclusions of this study: excellent teachers develop their abilities through constant self-evaluation, reflection, and the willingness to change.

Can we learn from the insights of highly effective teachers?

We can, but we may have to learn a lot about "teaching with your mouth shut," as Don Finkel put it in the wonderful title to his book, recognizing that teaching is not just delivering lectures but anything we might do that helps and encourages students to learn—without doing them any major harm.[1] That demands a fundamental conceptual shift in what we mean by teaching. If you ask many academics how they define teaching, they will often talk about "transmitting" knowledge, as if teaching *is* telling. That's a comforting way of thinking about it because it leaves us completely in control; if we tell them, we've taught them. To benefit from what the best teachers do, however, we must embrace a different model, one in which teaching occurs only when learning takes place. Most fundamentally, teaching in this conception is creating those conditions in which most—if not all—of our students will realize their potential to learn. That sounds like hard work, and it is a little scary because we don't have complete control over who we are, but it is highly rewarding and obtainable.

Perhaps the biggest obstacle we face is the notion that teaching ability is somehow implanted at birth and that there is little we can do to change whether we have it or not. Our subjects struggled to learn how to create the best learning environments. When they failed to reach students, they used those failures to gain additional insights. Most important, because they subscribed to the learning rather than the transmission model of teaching, they realized that they had to think about ways to understand students' learning. That might include attention to how they explained something, but it always focused more broadly on a rich internal conversation: What do I mean by learning? How can I foster it? How can my students and I best understand and recognize its progress (and setbacks)? How can I know whether my efforts help or hurt?

Carol Dweck's work can apply here. Remember that she found that people who believe intelligence is fixed often develop a sense of helplessness, while those who believe that it is expandable with hard work are more likely to succeed. Professors who believe that teaching is primarily transmitting knowledge may think that success depends on fixed personality traits over which they have little control ("some people are just born good lecturers, but I'm not"). Because others—like the people we studied—conceive of teaching as fostering learning, they believe that if they understand their students and the nature and processes of learning better, they can create more successful environments.

Part of being a good teacher (not all) is knowing that you always have something new to learn—not so much about teaching techniques but about these particular students at this particular time and their particular sets of aspirations, confusions, misconceptions, and ignorance. To learn from the best teachers we must recognize that we can learn—and that we will still have failures. We will not reach all students equally, but there is something to learn about each one of them and about human learning in general.

Perhaps the second biggest obstacle is the simplistic notion that good teaching is just a matter of technique. People who entertain that idea may have expected this book to provide them with a few easy tricks that they could apply in their own classrooms. Such ideas make enormous sense if you have a transmission model, but it makes no sense if you conceive of teaching as creating good learning environments. The best teaching is often both an intellectual creation and a performing art. It is both Rembrandt's brush strokes and the genius of insight, perspective, originality, comprehension, and empathy that makes a Dutch Master. In short, we must struggle with the meaning of learning within our disciplines and how best to cultivate and recognize it. For that task, we don't need routine experts who know all the right procedures but adaptive ones who can apply fundamental principles to all the situations and students they are likely to encounter, recognizing when invention is both possible and necessary and that there is no single "best way" to teach. If we are to benefit from the insights and practices of outstanding teachers, we must move beyond the stage of "received knowers," expecting right answers—tricks of the trade—that we can employ blindly.

When John Sexton took the oath of office as the fifteenth president of New York University in 2002, he called for a new kind of professor in the twenty-first century. "We must recast our notion of what it means to accept the title of 'professor,'" he argued. The concept of the "tenured professor as an ultimate independent contractor" must give way to the view that faculty members in the university embrace community responsibilities for the "entire enterprise of learning, scholarship and teaching."

As Sexton recognized, that new professor supports and requires a new kind of university. Rather than thinking in terms of the traditional dichotomy of research and teaching, a separation that often paralyzed higher education in the twentieth century, we can begin to think of ourselves as a learning university concerned with the learning of both faculty (research) and students (teaching) and the ways in which the learning of one can benefit the other. The Learning University can sometimes mean that students participate in the research of their professors, or that they engage in their own investigations, but more broadly it means the creation of a community in which professors and students are engaged in rich intellectual conversations in a collegial environment. It is reflective of an attitude about students and their worth (whether those students are the ones Chad Richardson encountered in an open admissions university or the highly select scholars who enroll at Harvard and NYU).

It is a recognition that efforts to foster learning in others can stimulate our own greater understanding. It is a commitment on the part of the faculty to building and sustaining a community of learners. At its core, such a community is defined by engagement, by commitment of faculty and students to sustaining the community and its conversations.

The call to reject the dichotomy of teaching and research and to define anew what it means to be a professor has a certain moral dimension to it. It recognizes the inherent selfishness of concentrating only on the learning of faculty members and the ethical obligation to the development of our students, but it also has a practical quality. We cannot long sustain a learned community that pits one generation's achievements against the advancement of all others.

Yet we can't just say to faculty, teach more and better. If we are truly interested in defining a new university and a new professorate, we must recognize that there is something to know about human learning. Both the research and the theoretical literature on learning and teaching can inform how we design a course or any other educational experience. Disciplines can benefit both from vigorous epistemological inquiries into what it means to know in the field and from research on how people learn to think. Ultimately, that means that we benefit from the best teachers by doing something that many of them didn't. Not many of them did systematic examinations of the learning literature; they developed their insights from working with students. Yet the concepts they developed reflect well the conclusions of social and cognitive psychologists, educational anthropologists, sociologists, and other researchers. We must be willing to engage in the kind of reflection on experience that led our outstanding teachers to their wisdom, but it seems foolish to ignore the rich and growing body of research and theoretical work on learning. We wouldn't tolerate it if our students announced that they planned to stop studying in our disciplines and to draw all their conclusions from intuition or whim.

To create a new kind of professor who understands both the discipline and how it might be learned, we must change the way we develop young scholars and support existing ones. Dudley Herschbach has suggested that every dissertation should contain a chapter on how to help other people learn the subject of that study. Lee Shulman has proposed that departments require job candidates to conduct a seminar on their teaching philosophies.[2] We can also provide support for current professors. Colleges and universities can establish departments or institutes that study and advance university learning, academic entities whose faculty spend their time researching educational issues, thinking about their implications for the university educational enterprise, and helping their colleagues in other departments realize and benefit from the meaning of those studies.

Those institutes can develop research-based teaching initiatives in which they work with colleagues across the university to tackle problems. They might focus on why certain groups of students (defined by whatever demography) do not achieve the kind of learning expected, or about how to help all students achieve a new level of development. The initiative would refine the questions; explore the existing literature; and fashion a hypothesis about what might work, a program to implement that hypothesis, and a systematic assessment of the result, ultimately contributing to a growing body of literature on university learning.

Faculty for such institutes could come from traditional fields but develop specialized studies of learning in their own disciplines, or they might come from the learning sciences. By constituting such institutes as academic entities and the people who work in them as faculty members, colleges and universities can recognize the serious intellectual nature of their enterprise and hold them to the same rigorous standards for tenure and promotion that they impose on others. Such moves would also help attract some of the best minds in the academy into the enterprise, and encourage advanced scholars in each field occasionally to spend time thinking about and exploring these issues, serving as visiting scholars in the institutes. Several teaching centers have already emerged as prototypes for such departments.[3]

A number of forces prevail against ever winning for teaching the kind of intellectual respect bestowed upon the discovery of knowledge. For the last half century, much of the money for higher education has come through grants for research. The most successful and prestigious institutions have built their reputations with those dollars. In the rush to surpass the intellectual achievements of other countries, we have gambled on the learning potential of only two or three post-World War II generations of scholars, while often ignoring the needs of most of our students. It is difficult to maintain a democratic society with such policies. We can't even know for sure that our traditional methods of assessing learning have actually identified the most talented of potential scholars.

Yet there is a little secret that may still trump the antiteaching forces. Twice in the 1990s Syracuse University surveyed faculty and administrators at many of the leading research universities in the country, asking them what they thought about teaching and research.[4] On average, everybody along the line from professors, through department chairs, to deans, provosts, and presidents thought that both teaching and research were equally important to them, but everybody believed they put more stock in teaching than did the next person up the line. Professors thought their colleagues valued it more than did the chair, the chair more than the dean, and so forth. Presidents, provosts, and deans, meanwhile, believed that they cared far more about teaching than did the average faculty member. So the secret is out: everyone really does care about teaching, or at least says they do, or knows they should—even within the research university. Now it's time we did something about that little secret.

APPENDIX

NOTES

ACKNOWLEDGMENTS

INDEX

APPENDIX:
HOW THE STUDY WAS CONDUCTED

When I was an undergraduate in the early 1960s, I became fascinated with the highly effective teachers I encountered because they made such a strong difference in my own personal and intellectual growth. When I was a sophomore, I started talking with a handful of my instructors about what they did and why they did it, and those conversations had an enormous influence on my thinking as I subsequently acquired a Ph.D. in U.S. history and joined a university faculty. Like most college and university professors, I had no formal preparation for helping anyone else learn. My research and published scholarship centered on the development of U.S. foreign policy in the Middle East, but that provided little if any understanding of how I might best help someone else learn to think and understand like a good historian. In my first fifteen years of teaching, I read little of the research or theoretical literature on learning and teaching. In the early 1980s, however, when I was a professor of history and director of the University Honors Program at the University of Texas—Pan American, I finally began a systematic study of that literature, primarily in connection with efforts to establish a national history teaching center. At the same time, I was interested in identifying the best teachers to offer classes in the honors program. I began sitting in on some classes, interviewing students, reviewing professors' syllabi, and talking to some colleagues about their teaching.

At the time, I didn't conceive of those actions as part of an ongoing study, but when I arrived at Vanderbilt in 1986 and started the Center for Teaching in the College of Arts and Science, I realized that I had learned a lot from that review of outstanding teachers. I also realized that additional study could enhance my work in the Center. Thus I began a systematic effort to identify and examine highly effective university and college teachers.

Marsha Faye Marshall, the only other person involved in the study at that point, came to it after teaching in a private grade school and managing continuing medical education courses in the Vanderbilt Medical School (and later executive education courses for the Kellogg School of Management). She helped spell out the criteria we would use in identifying subjects and some of the questions used in both formal and informal interviews. She also helped analyze videotapes of interviews and formal presentations from the subjects, looking for patterns in their discussions. After I moved to Northwestern in 1992 and became director of the Searle Center for Teaching Excellence, James Lang joined the study while he was finishing a Ph.D. in English literature and subsequently as assistant director of the Center in the late 1990s. He conducted some of the interviews and helped analyze and synthesize the data that were emerging from them. He analyzed, in particular, the ideas emerging about the evaluation of teaching, and he helped synthesize them into the form presented in the last chapter. Several graduate students in higher education who studied with the late Robert Menges, including Dorothy Cox, helped conduct interviews of subjects and shape some of the emerging conclusions.

To identify *potential* candidates, we relied primarily on the following sources of information: interviews with hundreds of students about teachers who had made a significant and positive difference in their intellectual and personal development, conversations with professors about colleagues who had strong reputations for helping students achieve high learning, lists of major teaching award winners, and, in later years, recommendations from professors and students that a particular person merited inclusion. In the mid-1990s, we solicited nominations from participants in several e-mail discussion groups. In 1996, we began conducting three-day national and international conferences on the initial results of the study, and those conferences brought increased publicity to the enterprise and additional nominations from throughout the United States and Australia.

Once we identified a potential subject, we began to collect information that could help us determine whether there was sufficient evidence to merit that person's inclusion. Student ratings on global or outcome questions, if available, had to be exceptionally high, but high ratings alone were not sufficient. Other evidence had to exist that demonstrated that the professor regularly fostered exceptional learning. The nature of that evidence varied with discipline and individual, but it might include the syllabus, examinations, methods of evaluation, observations of the teaching, self-reports (for evidence about the quality of the learning objectives), examples of students' work, performance on departmental examinations, students' subsequent performance in other classes, and interviews with students (for evidence about success in fostering advanced learning). See Chapter 1 for specific examples. Low ratings, however, meant automatic exclusion from the study, on the basis that no matter what kind of learning had taken place, the low rating left strong evidence of student alienation that could corrupt learning and discourage additional study in the field.

All candidates entered the study on probation until we had sufficient evidence that their approaches fostered remarkable learning. Ultimately, the judgment to include someone in the study was based on careful consideration of his or her learning objectives, success in helping students achieve those objectives, and ability to stimulate students to have highly positive attitudes toward their studies. We wanted to know that the teacher was successful in reaching most, if not all, the students, and in helping an unusually high number of them achieve what we could regard as exceptionally advanced levels of learning. As the project progressed, we experienced a revolution of rising expectations, such that people selected later in the study generally had to meet higher standards than those selected earlier. We could not, however, reduce to a formula our decision about who was in and who was out any more than we could do so in evaluating a scholarly manuscript in history.

We chose to include and study a total of sixty-three different teachers. The method of inquiry often resembled that of the investigative journalist or the narrative historian in that we were looking primarily at qualitative evidence from a variety of sources, drawing conclusions from the testimonies we heard and documents we read, and weaving them into a comprehensive story rather than doing statistical analyses of quantitative data. We utilized six principal sources of information about our subjects: (1) formal or informal interviews; (2) public presentations or written discussions of their ideas about teaching; (3) syllabi, assignment sheets, statements of grading policy, lecture notes, and other written materials that the subjects prepared in connection with the teaching of particular courses; (4) observations of their teaching in the classroom or elsewhere, including in some cases video recordings of those sessions; (5) students' products, including their attitudes, conceptions (collected in interviews, small group analyses, and rating forms), and academic work (papers, examinations, projects, performances, and so on); and (6) colleagues' comments, usually to provide judgments of learning objectives and the subsequent reputations of students of the people we studied. We utilized five or six types of sources with the thirty-five subjects we studied most closely, and at least two kinds of sources with each of the remaining twenty-eight people. We observed an entire course for six of the subjects, and portions of courses from thirty-five others.

Most of the formal interviews were recorded. The informal interviews consisted of conversations, often quite casual, that we had with some subjects. We utilized informal discussions for both logistical reasons (because formal interviews were difficult to arrange) and as a result of methodological considerations. We wanted to see if the patterns of responses would be different in what appeared to our subjects to be informal conversations about their teaching, telling us things that didn't emerge when we sat other people down in front of a video camera. We discovered that many of the subjects in those informal arrangements seemed more candid, less guarded than did some of their colleagues in the formal interviews. Whether formal or informal, those conversations centered around four areas of inquiry: What are the learning objectives you have for your students? How do you foster the achievement of those objectives? What evidence do you have about students' successes in achieving those objectives? What evidence do you have that your methods contribute significantly to the learning that takes place? When we asked professors to offer a public explanation of their teaching, we provided the same broad questions as guides for their talks or articles.

The specific questions under each of these four broad types of inquiries varied with discipline and individual and evolved over time as we developed better insights from early interviews and conversations. Some lines of inquiry emerged in the Peer Review Project in which Northwestern and eleven other institutions participated under the guidance of the American Association for Higher Education from 1994 to 1998. Here are some of the questions we used: How would you describe your understanding of how humans learn? What happens cognitively when students learn something new? How do you prepare to teach? What questions do you ask yourself as you prepare a lesson, a course, or any other learning experience for students? What do you promise students in your teaching? What will they be able to do intellectually, physically, or emotionally as a result of studying with you? What do you expect of their learning if you are to regard it as successful? What do you do when you teach? What are your primary teaching methods? Where does that teaching usually take place? What do you do that is intended to help and encourage students to learn? Are there any good metaphors for your approach to teaching? How would you describe your relationship with students? What kinds of things do you like most about the students you have taught? What have you liked least? What, if any, major problems do students face in learning from you? What, if any, major problems do you face in helping them to learn? How do you know when you have done a good job of teaching? How do you check your progress and evaluate your own efforts? Do you have any evidence about the success of your teaching?

We also asked the following questions in reference to specific courses: How does the course begin? Why does it begin where it does? What do you and your students do as the course unfolds? How does it end? Why does it end as it does? What do you lecture about or lead discussions around? What are the key assignments and means of evaluating student work? What do you want to persuade your students to believe? Or question? Or do you want them to develop new appetites or dispositions? Does your course teach students how scholars work in your field—the methods and values that shape how knowledge claims are made and adjudicated within your field? Does it teach them the logic of your discipline, that is, how scholars in your field reason from evidence, what concepts they employ, what assumptions they make, and what implications their conclusions have? What big questions will your course help students answer? What intellectual abilities (or qualities) will it help students develop? What do you expect students to find particularly fascinating about your course? Where will they encounter their greatest difficulties of either understanding or motivation? How has the course evolved over time? Is your course like a journey, a parable, a game, a museum, a romance, a concerto, an Aristotelian tragedy, an obstacle course, one or all or some of the above? How does your metaphor(s) illuminate key aspects of your course?

Our primary goal was simply to get people talking about their teaching, telling us stories about their classes. Our method was a lot like paddling a canoe downstream; we occasionally stuck our oar in the water to keep from running aground and to make sure we explored the main channels of interest. Like any good historians who might employ oral history research techniques, we subsequently sought corroborating evidence, usually in the form of something on paper (examples of student work, copies of examinations or assignment sheets, the syllabus, and so on), but sometimes from video recordings of individual classes.

In a small group analysis (SGA), we met with the students in the absence of the professor (usually at the end of a class session), divided them into pairs or small groups, and asked each pair or group to spend eight to ten minutes discussing three questions: (1) What has been successful in fostering your learning? (2) What changes in the structure of the class or the way the class is conducted would better foster your learning? and (3) How would you characterize the nature of your learning in the class? We also asked them to take notes on their discussions. When time was up, we brought all students back together to get reports from the groups. At that point, we could do two things that we could not do on a written instrument: clarify (ask follow-up questions) and verify (determine whether a given report reflected everyone's views or a division in the ranks). The entire procedure usually took approximately twenty minutes. We would take notes on the group reports and collect the notes students took in their discussions.

We read and reread the materials that we had on paper (syllabi, course materials, notes from SGAs, and conversations) and watched and rewatched videotapes of interviews and of classes many times to identify broad and dominant patterns. We recognized that not everyone used the same language to describe the same objectives and practices. Our own acquaintance with the research and theoretical literature helped us to pick through the terminologies and scenes we encountered, to give practices and ways of thinking common names, and to recognize the patterns that unfolded before us, but we also tried to let the texts we collected from and about our subjects dictate the emerging conclusions. To do so, we often tried to write individual stories about people in the study and then to discuss what those stories had in common.

On the basis of a careful and informed examination of the evidence, we can argue that all sixty-three people we identified experienced exceptional success in helping and encouraging their students to achieve remarkable learning results. Because we were not running a contest in which we surveyed large numbers of faculty members or a randomly selected cross-section to pick winners, we cannot say for certain, however, that there are not others who had equal or even superior success. A demographic report on the group, therefore, would provide little meaningful information and might even leave false impressions. If we studied more men than women, for example, that might reflect little more than that there are more men than women teaching at the college level. If we saw higher percentages of women in our group than in the general population of faculty members, that could be coincidental. Seven people had taught less than ten years (none less than five); another twenty-two, less than fifteen; and another five, less than twenty. All the others had taught for more than twenty years. All but a dozen of the professors we identified taught in research institutions, but that simply reflects where we were located and does not say anything about where most good teachers are employed.

Significantly, the methods we identified as most effective were used in both highly selective and open-admissions schools, suggesting to us that some fundamental principles prevailed and worked well regardless of the academic qualifications of the students. We looked at people from forty different disciplines, with generally equal balance between humanities, social science, and science-mathematics-engineering. Five were from the performing arts; ten taught in graduate professional schools, and two of those also taught undergraduates; fifty-five taught undergraduates; and more than half of those also taught graduate students. None of this suggests anything about where good teachers are likely to be found, but it does reflect the breadth of the study.

Our inquiry consisted primarily of a series of case studies in which we were trying to tell both the collective and, in some cases, the individual stories of the highly effective teachers we discovered. We offer these results both as evidence that certain approaches work effectively and as a theoretical foundation for additional inquiries. Future studies can begin to test methods against each other in a manner that we employed in only one case. In that example (the biologists who developed Advanced Conceptual Workshops—see Chapter 4), we were able to compare the accomplishments of matched pairs of students, some who were allowed to participate after volunteering and other volunteers who were denied the treatment and remained in other, more conventional, learning environments. In that case, we were able to consider extensive statistical analyses to compare academic performances of participants, a control group, and a group of non-volunteers.[1]

Our thorniest methodological question remained how we would define "exceptional learning." We discovered that we could not develop a general definition that would fit all disciplines, but we also discovered that the ideas we heard from our subjects shaped our understanding of what "exceptional learning" might mean (and contributed to that revolution of rising expectations noted earlier). The closest we came was in terms of intellectual and personal development. In general, we thought of intellectual development as understanding a sizeable body of material, learning how to learn (to expand understanding), to reason from evidence, to employ various abstract concepts, to engage in conversations about that thinking (including the capacity to write about it), to ask sophisticated questions, and the habits of mind to employ all those abilities. Personal development meant understanding one's self (one's history, emotions, dispositions, abilities, insights, limitations, prejudices, assumptions, and even senses) and what it means to be human; the development of a sense of responsibility to one's self and others (including moral development); the capacity to exercise compassion; and the ability to understand and use one's emotions. It also meant the emergence of the habits of the heart to maintain and employ these developments.

NOTES

1. INTRODUCTION

1. All Lynn quotations from Robert Darden, ed., *What a World! Collected Essays of Ralph Lynn* (Waco, Tex.: Narrative Publishing, 1998).

2. A clear example of students' ability to perform without learning comes from studies done in physics which demonstrate that students in an introductory course can learn how to solve physics problems even though they retain the same fundamentally mistaken ideas about motion that they brought with them to the course. See Chapter 2 for more on these studies.

3. Ference Marton and Roger Säljö, "On Qualitative Differences in Learning—2: Outcome as a Function of the Learner's Conception of the Task," *British Journal of Educational Psychology* 46 (1976): 115–127.

4. Donald H. Naftulin, John E. Ware, Jr., and Frank A. Donnelly, "The Doctor Fox Lecture: A Paradigm of Educational Seduction," *Journal of Medical Education* 48 (1973): 630–635.

5. Robert M. Kaplan, "Reflections on the Doctor Fox Paradigm," *Journal of Medical Education* 49 (1974): 310–312; quotation from p. 311.

6. See, for example, Peter A. Cohen, "Student Ratings of Instruction and Student Achievement: A Meta-analysis of Multisection Validity Studies," *Review of Educational Research* 51 (1981): 281–309; Judith D. Aubrecht. "Are Student Ratings of Teacher Effectiveness Valid?" *IDEA Paper*, no. 2, November 1979 (Manhattan, Kans.: Kansas State University, Center for Faculty Evaluation and Development); Robert T. Blackburn and Mary Jo Clark, "An Assessment of Faculty Performance: Some Correlates between Administrator, Colleague, Student and Self-Ratings," *Sociology of Education* 48 (1975): 242–256; Larry Braskamp, Frank Costin, and Darrel Caulley, "Student Ratings and Instructor Self-Ratings, and Their Relationship to Student Achievement," *American Educational Research Journal* 16 (1979): 295–306; Frank Costin, William Greenough, and Robert Menges, "Student Ratings of College Teaching: Reliability, Validity, and Usefulness," *Review of Educational Research* 41 (1971): 511–535; Frank Costin, "Do Student Ratings of College Teachers Predict Student

Achievement?" *Teaching of Psychology* 5 (1978): 86–88; P. C. Abrami, S. d'Apollonia, and P. A. Cohen, "Validity of Student Ratings of Instruction: What We Know and What We Do Not," *Journal of Educational Psychology* 82 (1990): 219–231; K. A. Feldman, "Instructional Effectiveness of College Teachers as Judged by Teachers Themselves, Current and Former Students, Colleagues, Administrators, and External (Neutral) Observers," *Research in Higher Education* 30 (1989): 137–194; K. A. Feldman, "The Association between Student Ratings of Specific Instructional Dimensions and Student Achievement: Refining and Extending the Synthesis of Data from Multisection Validity Studies," *Research in Higher Education* 30 (1989): 583–645.

7. Kenton Machina, "Evaluating Student Evaluations," *Academe* 73 (1987): 19–22.

8. Herbert W. Marsh, "Experimental Manipulations of University Student Motivation and Effects on Examination Performance," *British Journal of Educational Psychology* 54 (1984): 206–213.

9. Nalini Ambady and Robert Rosenthal, "Half a Minute: Predicting Teacher Evaluations from Thin Slices of Nonverbal Behavior and Physical Attractiveness," *Journal of Personality and Social Psychology* 64 (1993): 431–441.

10. We believe these conclusions transcend much of the recent debate over traditional and innovative approaches to teaching, about passive or active learning, or about a "sage on the stage" versus a "guide by the side." They help explain why some professors stimulate learning using what others would regard as outmoded pedagogies while others fail miserably with the latest rage, and still others do the opposite. They speak to a higher set of considerations that ask not whether one has used the latest technologies and methodologies but about the kind of sustained and substantial influence the teaching has on the way students think, act, or feel.

11. For an introduction to some of this learning research, see John D. Bransford, Ann L. Brown, and Rodney R. Cocking, eds., *How People Learn: Brain, Mind, Experience and School* (Washington, D.C.: National Academy Press, 1999). See also notes to Chapter 2.

2. WHAT DO THEY KNOW ABOUT HOW WE LEARN?

1. Ibrahim Abou Halloun and David Hestenes, "The Initial Knowledge State of College Physics," *American Journal of Physics* 53 (1985): 1043–1055. See also Ibrahim Abou Halloun and David Hestenes, "Common

Sense Concepts about Motion," *American Journal of Physics* 53 (1985): 1056–1065.

2. Halloun and Hestenes, "Common Sense Concepts about Motion," quotation from p. 1059.

3. For further examples and discussions of this phenomenon in physics, see Jose P. Mestre, Robert Dufresne, William Gerace, Pamela Hardiman, and Jerold Touger, "Promoting Skilled Problem Solving Behavior among Beginning Physics Students," *Journal of Research in Science Teaching* 30 (1993): 303–317; Lilian C. McDermott, "How We Teach and How Students Learn," in Harold I. Modell and Joel A. Michael, eds., *Promoting Active Learning in the Life Science Classroom* (New York: The New York Academy of Sciences, 1993), pp. 9–19; and Sheila Tobias, *Revitalizing Undergraduate Science: Why Some Things Work and Most Don't* (Tucson: Research Corporation, 1992).

4. Kim A. McDonald, "Science and Mathematics Leaders Call for Radical Reform in Calculus Teaching." *Chronicle of Higher Education*, November 4, 1987, p. 1.

5. Edward L. Deci, "Effects of Externally Mediated Rewards on Intrinsic Motivation," *Journal of Personality and Social Psychology* 18 (1970): 105–115.

6. See Richard deCharms and Dennis J. Shea, *Enhancing Motivation: A Change in the Classroom* (New York: Irvington Publishers, 1976).

7. Edward L. Deci and Joseph Porac, "Cognitive Evaluation Theory and the Study of Human Motivation," in Mark R. Lepper and David Greene, eds., *The Hidden Costs of Reward: New Perspectives on the Psychology of Human Motivation* (Hillsdale, N.J.: Lawrence Erlbaum, 1978), pp. 149–176; quotation from p. 149.

8. Deci, "Effects of Externally Mediated Rewards on Intrinsic Motivation"; quotation from p. 107.

9. See J. Condry and J. Chambers, "Intrinsic Motivation and the Process of Learning," in *The Hidden Costs of Reward*, pp. 61–84; and T. S. Pittman, J. Emery, and A. K. Boggiano, "Intrinsic and Extrinsic Motivational Orientations: Reward-Induced Change in Preference for Complexity," *Journal of Personality and Social Psychology* 42 (1982): 789–797.

10. Melissa Kamins and Carol Dweck, "Person versus Process Praise and Criticism: Implications for Contingent Self-Worth and Coping," *Developmental Psychology* 35 (1999): 835–847.

11. See, for example, Carol S. Dweck, "Motivational Processes Affecting

Learning," *American Psychologist* 41 (1986): 1040–1048; and Carol W. Dweck and E. L. Leggett, "A Social-Cognitive Approach to Motivation and Personality," *Psychological Review* 95 (1988): 256–273.

12. In the 1980s, Susan Bobbitt Nolen studied children doing expository reading and noticed that if they had as their chief goal learning for "its own sake" (what she called "task orientation"), they were likely to use and value deep processing strategies in that reading. If the learners wanted primarily to do better than anyone else in the class (in her terms, "ego orientation"), they often used less sophisticated strategies, tending to engage in a superficial reading. See Susan Bobbitt Nolen, "The Influence of Task Involvement on the Use of Learning Strategies" (paper delivered at the Annual Meeting of the American Educational Research Association, Washington, D.C., April 20–24, 1987); Susan Bobbitt Nolen and Thomas M. Haladyna, "Personal and Environmental Influences on Students' Beliefs about Effective Study Strategies," *Contemporary Educational-Psychology* 15 (1990): 116–130.

13. Richard Light, *The Harvard Assessment Seminars* (Cambridge, Mass.: Harvard University, Graduate School of Education and Kennedy School of Government, 1990), pp. 8–9.

14. Robert de Beaugrande, "Knowledge and Discourse in Geometry: Intuition, Experience, Logic," *Zeitschrift für Phonetik, Sprachwissenschaft und Kommunikationsforschung* 6 (1991): 771–827; and *Journal of the International Institute for Terminology Research* 3/2 (1992): 29–125; quotation from the on-line version at *http://beaugrande.bizland.com/Geometry.htm*.

15. See William G. Perry, Jr., *Forms of Intellectual and Ethical Development in the College Years: A Scheme* (New York: Holt, Rinehart and Winston, 1970); William G. Perry, Jr., "Cognitive and Ethical Growth: The Making of Meaning," in Arthur W. Chickering, ed., *The Modern American College* (San Francisco: Jossey-Bass Publishers, 1990), pp. 76–116; Mary Field Belenky, Blythe McVicker Clinchy, Nancy Rule Goldberger, and Jill Mattuck Tarule, *Women's Ways of Knowing: The Development of Self, Voice, and Mind* (New York: Basic Books, 1986).

16. Blythe McVicker Clinchy, "Issues of Gender in Teaching and Learning," *Journal of Excellence in College Teaching* 1 (1990): 52–67; quotation from pp. 58–59.

17. Ibid., p. 59.

18. Ibid., p. 63.

19. Ibid., p. 65.

3. HOW DO THEY PREPARE TO TEACH?

1. Ernest Boyer's 1990 work *Scholarship Reconsidered* has popularized the idea of teaching as scholarship, but long before that book appeared, many of the teachers reflected its central thinking, with one important distinction. Boyer's essay and much of the subsequent "teaching as scholarship" imply that teaching is important because it is a form of scholarship, almost as if the word itself renders certain values to the act of helping someone else learn. For the teachers we studied, however, teaching is important not because it is scholarship but because it can make significant contributions to other people and to the path of intellectual (and sometimes artistic) development in the world. It requires attention from scholars (and in some fields, artists) because it involves serious intellectual (or artistic) work, a line of thinking to which scholars (or artists) are often uniquely prepared to contribute. This notion of what still might be called the "scholarship of teaching" recognizes the essential role for intellectuals in teaching while avoiding the often fatuous debate over whether it should fall under the same language traditionally reserved for the discovery of knowledge and its publication.

2. Chad Richardson, *Batos, Bolillos, Pochos, and Pelados: Class and Culture on the South Texas Border* (Austin: University of Texas Press, 1999).

4. WHAT DO THEY EXPECT OF THEIR STUDENTS?

1. In raising this question, Steele was confronting ideas that Kenneth Clark had developed in the 1930s and 1940s and that Thurgood Marshall had used in his plea before the Supreme Court in the landmark desegregation case of 1954, *Brown vs. the Board of Education of Topeka.* Clark had argued that because our racist society had discriminated against black children and had even segregated them into separate schools, it had taught them that they were inferior. Racism and discrimination had, as Earl Warren put it in his famous opinion in the Brown case, generated among the victims of the prejudice "a feeling of inferiority . . . that may affect their hearts and minds in a way unlikely ever to be undone." In short, the Clark theory held, if society keeps telling you that you are inferior, you are likely to believe it yourself. While Steele recognized that impact, he also saw that most African American students he encountered had a strong sense of self-worth and simply directed their energies into domains other than academics. His research, however, sought to explain the performance of those

who remained "attached to the domain," who continued to strive but still often failed.

2. He used the advanced portion of the Graduate Record Examination in mathematics to test two comparable groups of women, both with good undergraduate records in math courses. For one group, he made no special effort, and that group did far worse on the examination than did their male counterparts. For the other group, he convinced them before they took the examination that there would be no gender differences, and there were none. See Claude M. Steele, "Thin Ice: 'Stereotype Threat' and Black College Students" (August 1999); available online at *http://www.theatlantic.com/issues/99aug/9908stereotype.htm*.

3. But were the students who thought it was a test of ability thinking about the racial stereotypes? Apparently so. The researchers gave both groups a word game in which two letters were missing from each of a long list of words. They could complete each word in a variety of correct ways, some of which were connected with the concept of race. Students who thought their abilities were under scrutiny finished the letters with far more "racial" words than did the other group. Steele, "Thin Ice."

4. When Margaret Shih and her colleagues at Harvard tackled the issue, they tested the possible interplay between positive and negative stereotypes. Popular beliefs hold that women are weak at mathematics but Asian Americans are good at it. What about Asian American women? The Harvard researchers gave three groups of female Asian American college students a math test. Before each test they asked the women to fill out a questionnaire about themselves and general student issues. For the first group, they inserted a single question to remind them of their ethnicity. The second group didn't have that question, but had one to remind them of their gender, while the third group had neither of those questions. Even though all three groups should have performed the same, the one that had the subtle reminder of ethnicity did substantially better than did the other two, while the students who had the gender question did the worst. Margaret Shih, Todd L. Pittinsky, and Nalini Ambady, "Stereotype Susceptibility: Identity Salience and Shifts in Quantitative Performance," *Psychological Science* 10 (1999): 80–83.

5. Steele, "Thin Ice."

6. Paul Baker, *Integration of Abilities: Exercises for Creative Growth* (New Orleans: Anchorage Press, 1977), p. 4.

7. Ibid., p. 19.

8. Because of the years of failure, the number of minority students who bothered to sign up for the course had steadily diminished. Consequently, the program accepted all of the minority students who volunteered and paired them for study purposes with historic matches—minority students who had taken the course in previous years. Such comparisons were justified because the course had not changed appreciably and the same six professors were still teaching the course.

9. Arnold Arons, "Critical Thinking and the Baccalaureate Curriculum," *Liberal Education* 71 (1985): 141–157.

10. Kenneth Seeskin, "A Few Words about Teaching Intellectual History," *The Class Act* (January 1996), p. 1. Available online at *http://president.scfte.northwestern.edu/ClassAct_96_Jan.html.*

11. For logistical reasons, she sometimes asks the students to take one of the cards randomly "and imagine that what is on the card is 'lost.'"

12. Claude M. Steele, "A Threat in the Air: How Stereotypes Shape Intellectual Identity," in Eugene Y. Lowe, ed., *Promise and Dilemma: Perspectives on Racial Diversity and Higher Education* (Princeton: Princeton University Press, 1999), pp. 116–118. Such a "Socratic strategy," he argues, secures "a safe teacher-student relationship in which there is little cost of failure and the gradual building of domain efficacy from small gains."

13. Baker, *Integration of Abilities*, p. XIII.

5. HOW DO THEY CONDUCT CLASS?

1. The basic ideas of natural critical learning have their roots in both the critical thinking and the active learning movements, complementing and extending the thoughts of both. While active learning recognizes that it is best to have people involved in their own learning, natural critical learning recognizes that the action is most effective if the learner decides to do it because she thinks it will help her satisfy a need to know, help solve a problem that she regards as important, intriguing, or beautiful—not simply because someone told her to go talk with her neighbor. Whereas critical thinking defines learning in terms of the ability of students to reason through problems, natural critical learning defines ways in which they can develop the ability to do so.

2. The method described here of distributing written material must be employed with care. Students must walk away from the experience convinced that they derived something valuable that they could not get

elsewhere. Thus, merely distributing portions of a textbook and asking students to spend the class period discussing those passages probably wouldn't work very well.

3. A neuron is more than just a cell in a brain, of course, but she begins with a simple concept to help students build their own explanation.

4. They understood and used the rich and unique vocabulary of oral communication, where a gesture—a wry smile or even a raised eyebrow—can sometimes substitute for words, reminding an audience of a point already articulated. They used their voices to put a human face on information and ideas, conveying enthusiasm and interest, zeal for knowledge, and appreciation of other perspectives.

5. Comedians call this a "release," a signal to laugh. For Groucho Marx, it was the flick of his cigar; for Johnny Carson, pulling on his cuffs. In the classroom, such devices are signals to think. Thanks to Ann Woodworth for pointing out these examples and the analogy.

6. Sometimes, contrasting intentions stood out like a sore thumb. Some large lecture halls, for instance, have wireless lavaliere microphones available for professors to use to amplify their voices with the help of built-in sound systems. We noticed that in those rooms some teachers strapped on the supporting microphones and others did not. Yet the pattern of who did and who didn't had little to do with the power of anyone's naked voice. The best teachers tended to use them; weaker teachers did not (with some important exceptions). When we asked people on both sides of this divide why they did what they did, the responses were revealing. The users said they wanted their students to hear them, or they worried about the students in the back row. In contrast, the non-users often said they never thought about it, or that it was too much trouble. Some non-users claimed their voices were robust enough, even when they were clearly not, and seemed insulted that anyone would suggest otherwise. How they saw themselves seemed more significant than whether their students could hear.

7. I'm not suddenly arguing that good teaching is done only by telling and the use of formal lectures. All teachers explain things to their students (from assignments to ideas), and the most effective in fostering learning generally make better explanations than do others.

8. Feynman videotape is from the BBC program "Fun to Imagine." Reprinted with permission of Carl Feynman and Michelle Feynman.

9. Eric Mazur has made famous a variation on this technique in which he interrupts his lectures in physics by assigning small conceptual prob-

lems that students can do without making any calculations. He first asks students to work independently to pick the right answer from a list (multiple choice). He also asks students to rate their own confidence in their answer. After a few minutes, he asks the students to turn to a neighbor, compare and discuss answers, possibly change their answers, and re-rate their confidence. He discovered that both the number of right answers and the confidence ratings go up after this exercise. See Eric Mazur, *Peer Instruction: A User's Manual* (N.J.: Prentice-Hall, 1997).

6. HOW DO THEY TREAT THEIR STUDENTS?

1. See Paul Baker, *Integration of Abilities: Exercises for Creative Growth* (New Orleans: Anchorage Press, 1977).

2. Jerry Farber, *The Student as Nigger: Essays and Stories* (New York: Pocket Books, 1972).

7. HOW DO THEY EVALUATE THEIR STUDENTS AND THEMSELVES?

1. Meg Cullar, "Interview with Paul Baker," *Baylor Line* (Fall 2001), pp. 46–49; quotation from p. 46.

2. "Rate the effectiveness of the teacher in challenging you intellectually," or "rate the effectiveness of the instructor in stimulating your interest in the subject."

3. That reconceptualized notion of a teaching portfolio, which we first proposed in a 1997 article, comes directly from the practices we observed in the self-examination that our subjects practice. See James Lang and Ken Bain, "Recasting the Teaching Portfolio," *The Teaching Professor* (December 1997), p. 1.

4. A teacher might, for example, help students learn complex ideas by exposing them first to simple explanations, then gradually, over several sessions, unfolding the complexity. An observer watching only the first iteration might believe that the teacher left students with overly simplified notions when, in fact, she may have employed a strategy that worked well.

5. Provide an overall rating of the instruction; provide an overall rating of the course; estimate how much you learned; rate the effectiveness of the teacher in challenging you intellectually, and rate the effectiveness of the instructor in stimulating your interest in the subject. We recommend using a six-point scale rather than a five-point scale for student responses because the former requires more discrimination from the student rater.

6. See, for example, Herbert W. Marsh and M. Dunkin, "Students' Evaluations of University Teaching: A Multidimensional Perspective," in J. C. Smart, ed., *Higher Education: Handbook of Theory and Research*, vol. 8 (New York: Agathon, 1992), pp. 143–233; and H. W. Marsh, "The Influence of Student, Course, and Instructor Characteristics in the Evaluations of University Teaching," *American Educational Research Journal*, 17 (1980): 219–237.

7. See, for example, George Howard and Scott Maxwell, "Do Grades Contaminate Student Evaluations of Instruction?" *Research in Higher Education* 16 (1982): 175–188.

EPILOGUE

1. Donald L. Finkel, *Teaching with Your Mouth Shut* (Portsmouth, N.H.: Heinemann, 2000).

2. That teaching philosophy would presumably explore the four questions we have considered throughout this book: What does it mean to learn the subject? How do we best foster that learning? How do students and faculty best understand the nature and progress of that learning? How can faculty members know whether their efforts are helping or hurting?

3. See, for example, *http://www.nyu.edu/cte/researchbased.html* and *http://president.scfte.nwu.edu/S2_research.html*.

4. Peter J. Gray, Robert C. Froh, and Robert M. Diamond, *A National Study of Research Universities on the Balance between Research and Undergraduate Teaching* (Syracuse, N.Y.: Center for Instructional Development, Syracuse University, 1992); Peter J. Gray, Robert M. Diamond, and Bronwyn E. Adam, *A National Study of the Relative Importance of Research and Undergraduate Teaching at Colleges and Universities* (Syracuse, N.Y.: Center for Instructional Development, Syracuse University, 1996); Robert M. Diamond and Bronwyn E. Adam, *Changing Priorities at Research Universities: 1991–1996* (Syracuse, N.Y.: Center for Instructional Development, Syracuse University, 1997).

APPENDIX

1. See W. K. Born, W. Revelle, and L. Pinto, "Improving Biology Performance with Workshop Groups," *Journal of Science Education and Technology* 11 (2002): 347–365.

ACKNOWLEDGMENTS

The study that spawned this book began in the 1980s, after I had spent more than fifteen years as a college history professor. It continued as I became the founding director of a series of university teaching centers at Vanderbilt, Northwestern, and New York University. Two people besides me played a significant role in its initiation, execution, and completion. Marsha Faye Marshall was there from beginning to end, assisting in every aspect of the research and playing a key role in formulating many of the conclusions. James Lang helped with research, writing, the formulation of conclusions, and a variety of other responsibilities. Long after he was no longer an active participant in the study, he urged me to continue the work.

To do the study we depended on the support of many colleagues who were not subjects of the study but nevertheless contributed significantly by helping to identify candidates and play sounding board to emerging notions. Friends and relatives played a part, too, as did the multitude of students who participated in Small Group Analyses or sat for interviews about their best and worst teachers. My children, Tonia and Marshall, and my daughter-in-law Alice were all in college in the early years of the study, and their experiences and reflections provided valuable stimuli to the thinking that emerged. In the final stages of the manuscript preparation, they made valuable suggestions about how to improve the work.

I first began to see the contours of what we came to call the "Natural Critical Learning Environment" as I talked to Tonia about her experience in living in a language dormitory at Vanderbilt. Thanks also to Al Masino, who shared some of his experience as an art student in Baltimore. I also want to thank Brena and John Walker, two great teachers in South Carolina, who read early portions of the manuscript and offered valuable suggestions. My editors, Elizabeth Knoll and Christine Thorsteinsson, provided many excellent suggestions in the final stages of the writing. Emma Rossi and Loni Leiva provided valuable assistance with the final preparation of the manuscript.

And, of course, thanks to all the fascinating people who populated the study and who spent time talking with us about their teaching or giving a public lecture at our request. Finally, I want to thank my parents, Jesse Lee Bain and Vera Brooks Bain, who taught in a half dozen or more small-town high schools and grade schools in Georgia and Alabama long before I came along, and who first taught me.

INDEX

Active learning, 18, 47, 62–67, 81–82, 93, 192, 197. *See also* Natural critical learning environment
Advanced Conceptual Workshops, 81, 189
African American students, 68, 70, 73, 79–83, 195
Ambady, Nalini, 14
Anatomy, teaching of, 29–30
Architecture, teaching of, 63–66
Arizona State University, 22
Arons, Arnold, 85–87
Aronson, Joshua, 70–71
Art history, teaching of, 104–105
Asian American students, 71, 79–83
Assessment of students, 19, 35, 60, 74, 94, 140, 151–162; formative, 18, 35, 57–58, 100, 109, 152, 157–162; criterion-referenced, 35, 152, 160; design of, 57, 151–161; self, 59, 163; norm-referenced, 152; learning-based approach to, 152, 155–163; performance-based approach to, 152–156, 159, 160; conceptions of, 163. *See also* Examinations; Grading
Assignments, 20, 47, 52, 54, 60, 75, 88, 107, 114, 128–129, 152
Astronomy, teaching of, 92

Baker, Paul, 2–3, 72, 74, 79, 97, 142, 157
Banking model, 29, 42, 83; transmitting knowledge and, 16, 26, 27, 29–30, 45, 52, 53, 173, 174; pouring information and, 52, 87, 115
Bell, Derrick, 145–149, 153
Besanko, David, 142, 143, 169
Billings, Josh, 27
Biology, teaching of, 2, 5–6, 29–30, 36, 79–82, 89–91, 106, 112, 127
Brown, Deborah, 105
Bulimic education, 41
Business, teaching of, 105, 140

Cannon, Charlie, 64–66, 106, 113
Case-based learning, 6, 18, 30, 89–91, 99, 104–106, 110, 132–134, 146–148
Case-based teaching, 99, 106, 132–133, 146
Chemistry, teaching of, 37, 95, 101, 115, 130, 144
Clinchy, Blythe McVicker, 42–45
Cohen, Geoffrey, 72–73, 76
Collaborative learning, 18, 53, 57, 64–66, 80–83, 95, 99, 107–109, 129
Commitments, 112–114
Community of learners, 20, 55, 113, 147–148, 153, 176
Conceptions of teaching, 17, 48–60, 67, 72, 74–79, 83–85, 88, 89, 95–97, 109, 126–128, 131, 139, 142–144, 152, 157, 162, 173–174
Connected knowers, 43–44
Construction of knowledge, 9, 26, 30, 31, 115

Motivation, 32–34, 38–43, 76–78;
    extrinsic, 32–35, 38, 47, 154–155,
    161; intrinsic, 32–35, 46–47, 161
Muir, Ed, 106

Native American students, 79–83
Natural critical learning environment,
    18, 47, 60, 99–100, 102–109,
    111–112, 113, 116–117, 132
Natural sciences, teaching of, 4, 8, 24,
    29, 53, 79–83, 89–92, 101, 127,
    143–144
Negative stereotypes, 69, 72–73, 96
Nelson, Craig, 40, 142
Neuroanatomy, teaching of, 91
Newton's laws of motion, teaching of,
    22–23, 32
New York University, 146, 175
Nonjudgmental responsiveness,
    96–97
Norden, Jeanette, 2, 5–6, 35–36, 51,
    89–92, 106, 107, 112, 116, 121, 126,
    127, 139, 152, 161, 164–165
Northwestern University, 2, 4, 5, 14,
    39, 79–82, 92, 93, 98

Op-ed pieces, 147–148

Pan American University, 60–63
Paradigms, 26–28, 30, 112
Peer Review Project, 185–186
Performance-avoiders, 40, 41
Performing arts, teaching of, 2, 6–7,
    92–94, 97, 142, 157
Perry, William, 42–43
Personal development, 9, 85, 89–92,
    94, 96, 146, 148–149, 164–165,
    189–190
Person praise, 34–35
Philosophy, teaching of, 87–88,
    100–102
Philpott, Tom, 3–4

Physics, teaching of, 22–23, 28, 32, 68,
    105, 123–124, 151
Pinto, Larry, 80–83
Plug and chug, 22, 24, 32, 94
Politics, teaching of, 109–112, 127
Preparing to teach, 17, 49–60, 99–103,
    109–116
Problem-based learning, 18, 132. *See
    also* Case-based learning; Natural
    critical learning environment
Procedural knowers, 43–45
Project-based learning, 64–66
Promising syllabus, 74–75
Psychology, teaching of, 128

Questions, using, 31, 36, 37, 39, 41,
    44–46, 50, 54, 55, 88, 89, 101–105,
    107, 108, 110, 130–132, 133, 157

Reading, teaching of, 52, 54, 56, 63,
    88–89, 106, 115, 127
Received knowers, 42–44, 175
Relationships, teacher-student, 18,
    135–136, 139–145, 148–149, 158
Rembrandt's brush strokes, 20–21,
    174
Research-based teaching initiative,
    177–178
Rhode Island School of Design, 63–66
Richards, Ann, 1
Richardson, Chad, 60–63, 106, 175
Rosenthal, Robert, 14

Saari, Donald, 38, 94, 102–103, 106,
    110, 113, 127, 131, 161
Sandel, Michael, 109–112, 127
Scholarship of teaching, 4, 17, 49, 169,
    195
Searle Center for Teaching Excellence,
    182
Seeskin, Ken, 87–88
Separate knowers, 43–44